Praise for *Baker Bettie's Better Baking Book*

"I wish I had this book when I started baking! It's not only a collection of amazing recipes, but it answers the 'why' to your baking questions."
—**Gemma Stafford**, chef, author, and host of *Bigger Bolder Baking*

"Kristin has given bakers of any skill level the essential baking handbook with this collection of tested recipes, thorough instructions, and detailed kitchen lessons."
—**Sally McKenney**, author of *Sally's Baking Addiction*

"Kristin is so knowledgeable about baking and makes it incredibly fun to learn the science behind it all. I would have loved this book when I was learning to bake because it breaks down so much about how baking works and how to become a better baker. A must-have on every baker's shelf!"
—**Liz Marek**, award-winning cake decorator, author, and host of the *Sugar Geek Show*

"If you're looking for a baking textbook, a master guide that explains everything you need to know about baking, *Baker Bettie's Better Baking Book* is it. Kristin answers all questions that could possibly arise from a recipe, whether they concern ingredients, equipment, or techniques. She accompanies methods with delectable base recipes that invite readers to experiment and get creative, and illustrates them with stunning step-by-step photographs. A beautifully written book that will no doubt be a staple for novices and more experienced bakers alike."
—**Vedika Luthra**, author of *52 Weeks, 52 Sweets*

Baker Bettie's

Better Baking Book

Baker Bettie's

Better Baking Book

Classic Baking Techniques and Recipes for Building Baking Confidence

Kristin Hoffman

mango
PUBLISHING GROUP

CORAL GABLES

Cover Design: Elina Diaz
Cover Photo: Kristin Hoffman
Interior Photos: Kristin Hoffman & Lisa Kay Creative Photography
Food Styling: Kristin Hoffman & Kelly Haines
Layout & Design: Elina Diaz

For permission requests, please contact the publisher at:
Mango Publishing Group
2850 S Douglas Road, 4th Floor
Coral Gables, FL 33134 USA
info@mangopublishinggroup.com

For special orders, quantity sales, course adoptions and corporate sales, please email the publisher at sales@mango.bz. For trade and wholesale sales, please contact Ingram Publisher Services at customer.service@ingramcontent.com or +1.800.509.4887.

Baker Bettie's Better Baking Book: Classic Baking Techniques and Recipes for Building Baking Confidence

Library of Congress Cataloging-in-Publication number: 2021942390
ISBN: (print) 978-1-64250-658-7, (ebook) 978-1-64250-659-4
BISAC category code: CKB004000, COOKING / Methods / Baking

Printed in the United States of America

To Chris,

Thank you for constantly lifting me up and loving me through the bright and dark parts of life. You are the best partner, cheerleader, dishwasher, and cheesecake taste tester I could ever ask for. I love you.

Contents

Foreword 17

Introduction 19

How to Use This Book 25

Part 1: Before You Start Baking 27

    Chapter 1 Baking Ingredients and Their Functions 29

    Chapter 2 Essential Baking Equipment 53

    Chapter 3 Common Baking Techniques and Terminology ... 59

    Chapter 4 Essential Rules of Baking 69

Part 2: Mixing Methods & Master Recipes 81

Chapter 5 Quick Breads 83

    The Muffin Mixing Method 85

    The Biscuit Mixing Method 103

Chapter 6 Cookies & Bars 119

    The One-Bowl Method 120

    The Creaming Method for Cookies 130

Chapter 7 Cakes 143

    The Blending Method 146

    The Creaming Method for Cakes 152

    The Angel Food Method 162

    The Chiffon Mixing Method 168

Chapter 8 Pies 181

    Crusts 184

    Fillings 194

    Toppings 212

Chapter 9 Yeast Breads 225

    The Stages of Making Bread 228

Chapter 10 Miscellaneous Techniques & Components 249

Baking Conversions 264

Acknowledgements 266

About the Author 267

Index 268

Recipes

Chapter 5: Quick Breads   83

Sweet Batter Bread Master Recipe   89
     Blueberry Coffee Cake Loaf/Muffins   90
     Lemon Poppy Seed Loaf/Muffins   90

Savory Batter Bread Master Recipe   93
     Parmesan Herb Bread   94
     Cheddar Dill Bread   94

Fruit *or* Veg Quick Bread Master Recipe   97
     Chocolate Chip Banana Bread/Muffins   98
     Zucchini Bread/Muffins   98
     Loaded Carrot Bread/Muffins   98
     Apple Spice Oat Bread/Muffins   98

Cornbread Master Recipe   101
     Jalapeno Cheddar Cornbread   102
     Smoky Chipotle Cornbread   102

Buttermilk Biscuit Recipe   107
     Garlic Cheddar Biscuits   109
     Fresh Herb Biscuits   109

Scone Master Recipe   111
     Blueberry Lemon Scones   113
     Cherry Almond Scones   113
     Strawberry Shortcakes   113

Soda Bread Master Recipe   115
     "Brown Bread" Soda Bread   116
     Currant and Caraway Soda Bread   116

Chapter 6: Cookies & Bars   119

Classic Fudgy Brownie Recipe   123
     Salted Caramel Pecan Brownies   124
     Spiced Hot Chocolate Brownies   124

Blondie Master Recipe   127
     Classic White Chocolate Walnut Blondies   128
     Funfetti Blondies   128

Shortbread Master Recipe   133
     Shortbread Cut-Out Cookies   134
     Shortbread Thumbprint Cookies   135
     Shortbread Crumb Bars   136
     Shortbread Tart or Pie Crust   136

Drop Cookie Master Recipe   139
   Monster Cookies   140
   Spiced Rum-Soaked Oatmeal Raisin   140
   Chewy Chocolate Chip Pecan Cookies   140

Chapter 7: Cakes   **143**

Classic Chocolate Cake Master Recipe   149
   Death by Chocolate Cake   150

Pound Cake Master Recipe   155
   Marble Pound Cake   156
   Crumb Cake   156

Classic White Cake   159
   Funfetti Cake   160
   Coconut Cake   160

Angel Food Cake Recipe   165
   Chocolate Angel Food Cake   166

Yellow Chiffon Cake Recipe   171
   Lemon Rosemary Cake   172
   Boston Cream Pie   172

Vanilla Buttercream Frosting Recipe   175
   Chocolate Buttercream   176
   Coconut Buttercream   176
   Citrus Buttercream (Lemon, Orange, or Lime)   176
   Peanut Butter Buttercream   176
   Berry Buttercream (Strawberry, Raspberry, or Cherry)   176

Cream Cheese Frosting Recipe   177
   Coconut Cream Cheese Frosting   177
   Lemon, Orange, or Lime Cream Cheese Frosting   177
   Maple Cream Cheese Frosting   177

Chapter 8: Pies   **181**

Traditional Pie Pastry   187
Cookie Crumb Crust Recipe   193
Shortbread Crust   194
Fruit Pie Filling Master Recipe   197
   Traditional Fruit Pie   198
   Fruit Cobbler   199
   Fruit Crisp or Crumble   199
Cheesecake Master Recipe   203
Pastry Cream Master Recipe   207

Cream Pie	208
Pastry Cream Fruit Tart	208
Fruit Curd Master Recipe	211
Swiss Meringue Recipe	217
Swiss Meringue Buttercream	218
Popular Pie Flavor Combinations	221
Banana Cream Pie	221
Berry Crisp	221
Chocolate Cream Pie	221
Coconut Cream Pie	221
Dutch Apple Pie	222
Lemon Meringue Pie	222
Peach Cobbler	222
Strawberry Rhubarb Pie	222

Chapter 9: Yeast Breads — 225

No-Knead Lean Dough Master Recipe	235
Rustic Boule	236
Focaccia Bread	237
Pizza Crust	238
Soft Sandwich Bread Master Recipe	241
Honey Whole Wheat Bread	243
Seeded Sandwich Bread	243
Enriched Dough Master Recipe	245
Filled Rolls	246
Cinnamon Rolls	247
Sticky Buns	247
Dinner Rolls	247

Chapter 10: Miscellaneous Techniques & Components — 249

Berry Sauce	250
Caramel Sauce	251
Chocolate Ganache	253
Ganache Frosting/Whipped Ganache	253
Truffles	254
Cake Glaze	254
Egg Wash	255
Fruit Glaze	255
Toasted Nuts *or* Coconut	256
Powdered Sugar Glaze	257

Citrus Glaze   258
Vanilla Glaze   258
Apple Cider Glaze   258
Almond Glaze   258

Streusel Topping   261
Oat Streusel   261
Nut Streusel   261

Whipped Cream Topping   263

Foreword

I think the first time I knew Kristin ("Baker Bettie") Hoffman was the real deal was when I saw how enthralled she was with pie crust: *What is the melting point of butter, and how does that affect pie dough? How will the consistency of pie crust change if you use vegetable shortening instead of butter?*

Let's just say I can relate.

I launched *Sally's Baking Addiction* in 2011 with the same massive dedication that Kristin has to perfecting recipes and understanding ingredients. I've tested, written, photographed, and published more than 1,000 from-scratch recipes in addition to authoring three bestselling cookbooks. I understand the importance of a well-tested and well-written recipe, and I take that responsibility very seriously. Kristin does too.

When she asked me to write this foreword for *Baker Bettie's Better Baking Book,* I felt immensely honored. Kristin and I started our baking careers around the same time, and what I admire most is her unending passion for recipe perfection. And we both agree that the greatest joy in the kitchen is teaching others what we've learned along the way (oh, and speaking of kitchen joys, don't wait another *second* to try her Chocolate Angel Food Cake on page 166).

As a trained chef and baking educator, Kristin values the backbone knowledge that successful baking requires. Her methods are approachable for *everyone*—beginner or advanced. In fact, she once told me that her recipe development always begins with the question, "What would someone who has never baked before need to know?" She delivers her recipes and content in such a way that anyone can gain the confidence to pick up a whisk and say, "Let's do this!"

When I was growing up watching my grandmother and mother in the kitchen, I learned firsthand the power of from-scratch baking. Not only how delicious it can be, but also how it brings people together. If you don't believe me, try the Fresh Herb Biscuits on page 109 and watch everyone magically appear for a taste!

Put simply, understanding *how to bake* is just as important as the recipes you choose. Luckily, this cookbook gives you both.

Sally McKenney, author and creator of *Sally's Baking Addiction*

Introduction

The path that I've taken to writing this book has been a winding one, and I'm excited that you are joining me on your own baking journey. I want you to know that, if you have never baked anything in your life and are completely intimidated by it, I have been there. If you already have some baking experience but are frustrated by all of the flops, I've definitely been there too. Or if you simply have a love for baking and are eager to continue learning everything you can about it, I am right there with you now!

Wherever you are in your baking journey, I wrote this book for you. I want to help you gain an understanding of how baking works so that you feel confident in the kitchen. Gaining knowledge of baking techniques and a little bit of baking science will give you the freedom to play in the kitchen. I want baking to feel as joyful for you as it has become for me.

Finding My Love for Baking

I grew up in Kansas, eating some of the most wonderful baked goods. My grandmother's strawberry rhubarb pie was always my favorite. And while I was very interested in eating all of these delicious baked goods, I was completely uninterested in actually doing any baking as a kid. It wasn't until college that my love for baking blossomed.

My first bake was the chocolate chip cookie recipe from the back of the bag. I distinctly remember using the big tub of margarine as the butter in the recipe because I truly did not know the difference. I also remember firmly packing as much flour as I could fit into my measuring cup. Looking back at these mistakes reminds me of how much a recipe assumes you already know.

I shared those cookies with my friends, and they all raved over them. I remember thinking, "Maybe I have a natural talent for baking!" Spoiler: I didn't. Even mediocre chocolate chip cookies taste pretty dang good to everyone, especially college kids.

Following that mild baking success came a series of baking flops. I found baking so frustrating and fussy, but I was eager to get better at it. I wanted to understand what all of these foreign-to-me instructions meant.

"What does 'fold in' mean? How do you fold a batter?"

"Why does this muffin recipe call for baking soda while this other one calls for baking powder?"

"Why does the butter need to be room temperature in my cookie dough but cold in my pie dough?"

I wished I could find all of these answers in one place. I scoured the internet and cookbooks to piece it all together.

When my baked goods turned out well, they brought a lot of joy to the people I shared them with. I wanted to continue being the bringer of joy. Most people can remember the excitement of waiting for chocolate chip cookies to come out of the oven in childhood. This shared nostalgia around baked goods naturally connects us to the people we share them with. I fell in love with creating that connection through food.

Baking Is a Science

As my love for baking grew, I became fixated on chocolate chip cookies, but every recipe I tried was a slight disappointment. Sure, they were good—chocolate chip cookies are always good. But I wanted *my* definition of the perfect cookie. For me, it is a thick cookie that is slightly crispy on the outside and chewy in the middle. I wanted it to have lots of texture and depth of flavor. None of the recipes I found delivered.

I dove into reading everything I could about how to create this perfect cookie and started to understand the science of baking. If I baked the cookies at a higher heat, they wouldn't spread out as much. If I used a higher ratio of brown sugar, I would get a chewier center. If I browned the butter, I would get a lot of nutty notes and a richer flavor profile. All of this brought me to developing my very first recipe—my Ultimate Chocolate Chip Cookie recipe (which you can find on BakerBettie.com).

Image by Lisa Kay Creative Photography

"The Cookies"

I took my first successful batch of "the cookies" to work with me. My coworkers loved them and encouraged me to start selling them. I opened an online cookie shop called "Sweet Chip Cookies" and listed my newly created cookies as the main item I sold. I also created a customizable listing, where you could tell me what *your* definition of the perfect cookie was and I would create it for you.

Did you want a thin and crispy cookie with dark chocolate chips and walnuts? How about a thick and chewy cookie with dried cranberries and white chocolate chips? This idea became a fast hit. Soon I had a full-blown online cookie shop, complete with a variety of my favorite flavors as well as a way to create your own.

This concept has been a common thread in my recipe development through the years and has carried over into this book. Throughout the chapters, you will find my base recipes along with very detailed tutorials for how to master them. You will also learn how to utilize these master recipes in a wide variety of ways and will be given the tools to adapt them for your own personal preferences.

Baker Bettie Is Born

Within a few months, my online cookie business had more orders than I could handle as a side hustle. I quickly realized that I did not want to be a production baker, but I still wanted a reason to be baking. So in 2011, I decided to start a baking blog, BakerBettie.com, to document all of the things I was learning and creating. At this point, maybe I should go ahead and tell you that my real name isn't Bettie. My name is actually Kristin. So who is "Baker Bettie?"

"Baker Bettie" is my alter ego for the blog, and over the years, she has become a part of me. I am Bettie *and* Kristin; we are one and the same. "Baker Bettie" brings a bit of nostalgia for the desserts and baked goods you might remember growing up with. I want the process of learning to bake to feel comforting and approachable. I think a warm retro feel helps with this. People remember their grandma mixing cookie dough in her Pyrex bowl, and they feel a bit more relaxed when they see me doing the same.

The more I wrote on my site, the more it grew, and I eventually started generating an income from it. The baking science pulled people in, and the trustworthy recipes and understandable directions kept them there.

Baker Bettie Goes to Culinary School

In 2013, I decided to commit to a career in food for good. I had worked in restaurants since age fourteen in practically every position possible, but I decided to enroll in culinary school at JNA Institute of Culinary Arts to begin my formal education. I had never felt so excited to go to a class as I did in culinary school.

Culinary school was a real turning point in the way I thought about baking. Up to this point, I had been learning to bake recipe by recipe. I wasn't really putting whole concepts together. However, in school, we would learn a mixing method or technique and then apply that to various types of cooking or baking. It was a revelation in building my baking confidence. It also affirmed my drive to help other new bakers learn in a simpler way.

Following culinary school, I worked as a private chef for a few years while still creating educational content online as "Baker Bettie," and my approach was really resonating with people. My passion for helping my readers become confident bakers grew larger, and I wanted to dedicate myself to it fully.

In 2018, I stepped away from my private chef job to teach as Baker Bettie full-time. Now I continue to create content on my website, create educational YouTube videos, and teach in-person baking workshops in the Chicago area. Additionally, I launched an online baking school, the Better Baking School, where I teach e-courses along with other experts in the field. I feel incredibly lucky to share my joy of baking with others as my everyday job.

How This Book Works

For the past few years, I have toyed with the idea of writing this book. I wanted to translate the approach of culinary school for the home baker. I felt confident that, if I could guide bakers through mixing methods, techniques, and approachable baking science, they would feel more confident with baking and love it as much as I do.

I have been teaching baking online for the last ten years, and it's a wonderful medium to connect with people from all over the world. But it is more difficult to guide bakers through a wide range of topics sequentially, which is why I'm ecstatic about sharing this book with you!

While you can dip in and out of this book for recipes, *I'm going to encourage you to go through this book sequentially from start to finish.* It is laid out to guide you through lessons that continue building on each other, so that you will finish this book with a great deal of baking confidence. *This is the book that I wish I had when I was first learning to bake.*

Part I lays out some important groundwork for everything that will follow. We cover basic ingredient functions, essential baking equipment, and important baking science that will apply to the chapters that follow.

Part II, dives into techniques, and master recipes. In this section, you learn specific mixing methods and the master recipes that utilize these methods. You will see how versatile these master recipes can be in creating a wide variety of baked goods.

Each chapter also covers key baking science that will help you identify what may have gone wrong if you ever have a baking mishap. Each of these chapters could be written into a book all by itself. My goal for you is to lay the groundwork for understanding the fundamentals of each topic, so you feel confident venturing beyond this book into more advanced techniques and recipes.

Thank you for trusting me to teach you. Let's dive in!

How to Use This Book

The best way to get the full experience of this book is to start at the beginning and work your way through. The material builds upon itself, and each section sets you up with more knowledge for your success with the next. I built the chapters and information in the exact order that I would cover if I were teaching an in-depth Fundamentals of Baking course.

However, I know this is not everyone's style and you may wish to jump into the recipes from the start. If this is you, it is helpful for you to know that *every recipe in this book is customizable*. These recipes are my masters that I start from when I am recipe developing.

Each recipe will list the base ingredients upfront that are needed to make the basic version of the baked good. Following the written instructions, you will also find a *flavor chart and/or flavor variation ideas* to help you create endless versions of your own! You will also be guided in how you can pair some of the master recipes together for even more versatility.

It is also helpful to note that all of the recipes utilize specific mixing methods and techniques that are covered in the material that precedes each one. If you are unfamiliar with a specific mixing method, or would like to brush up on the subject, I highly recommend looking at the pages prior to the recipe for step-by-step photos and key baking science tips that will ensure your success.

Most importantly, use this book to celebrate the joy of baking! Bake for those you love, bake for yourself, bake for important occasions, and just because. Every day is a good day to bake, and I hope you use this book to embrace that!

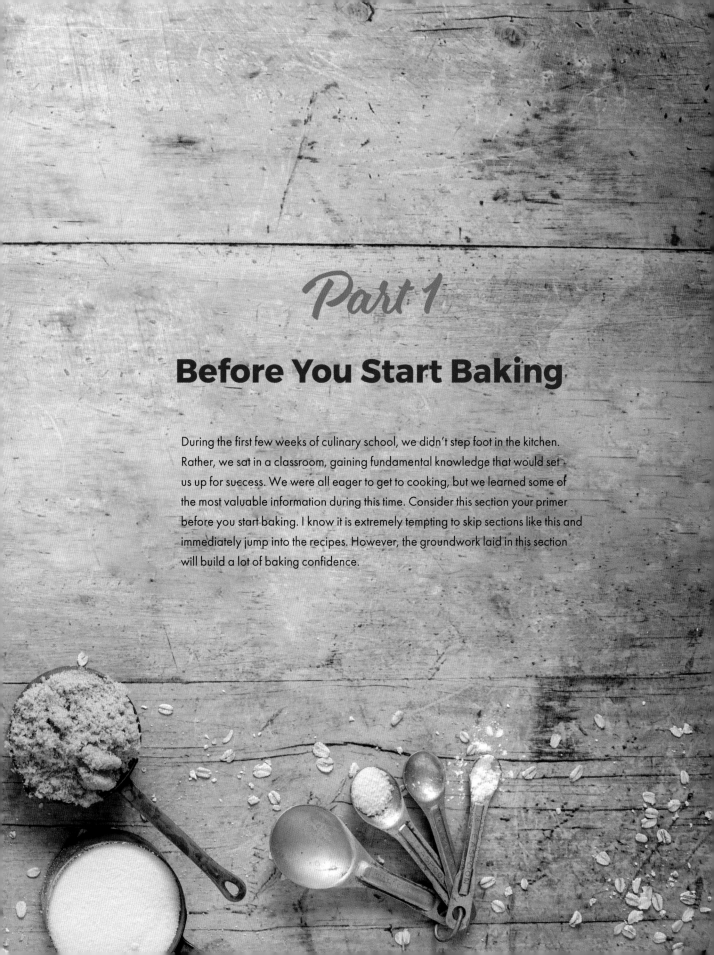

Part 1

Before You Start Baking

During the first few weeks of culinary school, we didn't step foot in the kitchen. Rather, we sat in a classroom, gaining fundamental knowledge that would set us up for success. We were all eager to get to cooking, but we learned some of the most valuable information during this time. Consider this section your primer before you start baking. I know it is extremely tempting to skip sections like this and immediately jump into the recipes. However, the groundwork laid in this section will build a lot of baking confidence.

1

Baking Ingredients and Their Functions

I believe one of the most underrated subjects when learning how to bake is understanding how ingredients function. Having some basic knowledge of the most-used ingredients and their purpose in baking is extremely helpful in troubleshooting, if you need to make a substitution, or if you ever want to create your own recipes.

Flour

In traditional baking, wheat flour is the most important ingredient. It builds the structure of most baked goods, and understanding how it functions is essential for better baking. Since this book is geared toward classic baking techniques, we will not be covering gluten-free flours in depth, as that is a topic that deserves a book all on its own.

Flour's Role in Baking

The main function of flour in baking is to build structure through the production of gluten. There are a few different kinds of wheat flour that are used in baking, but they all essentially serve the same function.

What is Gluten?

Wheat contains two proteins: glutenin and gliadin. When these proteins absorb water, they bond together, forming an elastic network called gluten. The more a dough or batter is mixed or kneaded, the stronger and more elastic the gluten network becomes.

When a dough or batter is baked, the gluten network stretches to contain gases in baked goods, allowing them to rise. A strong gluten network will produce baked goods with a lot of chew, such as bread, while a weak gluten network will produce baked goods that are light and tender, such as cake.

Whole Wheat Flour vs. White Flour

The wheat grain contains three parts: the bran, the germ, and the endosperm. Whole wheat flour is made by grinding the entire wheat grain. White flour is made from only the endosperm part of the wheat grain, which is pale in color and produces a softer flour.

Whole wheat flour is darker in color, more flavorful, and contains more nutrients than white flour. It does, however, have a coarser texture and is more absorbent than white flour, requiring a higher liquid ratio. The bran and germ present in whole wheat flour also work as little knives, cutting through gluten networks. Therefore, it is more difficult to build a strong gluten structure when working with whole wheat flour. This can lead to more dense and heavy baked goods.

Bleached vs. Unbleached Flour

In the US, white flour is also divided into two main categories: bleached and unbleached. When flour is first milled, it naturally has a slight yellow tint, which consumers do not find appealing. Therefore, flour either goes through a natural aging process or is chemically bleached. Both processes lighten the color and soften the texture of the flour.

Bleached flour is quicker to make than unbleached flour and is therefore usually less expensive. The chemical process also produces flour with a brighter white color, a finer texture, and weaker protein than unbleached flour. Some find that bleached flour also has a subtle flavor and smell that they do not prefer.

In general, either bleached or unbleached all-purpose flour can be used for most everyday baking and produce great results. However, bleached flour isn't the best option for making yeast bread, because it makes it more difficult to build a strong gluten structure. For this reason, I personally prefer to use unbleached flour for most of my baking, as I find it to be more versatile.

Varieties of Flour

Wheat flour is made in a wide range of varieties, depending on its intended use. The differences in the varieties depend on the type of wheat it is made from, how finely it is ground, and the protein content (since protein is what creates gluten). Most of the recipes in this book will be made with all-purpose flour, with a few exceptions.

For home bakers, I recommend keeping three types of flour on hand: all-purpose flour (preferably unbleached), bread flour, and cake flour. You might also want to add whole wheat flour to your lineup if you are interested in whole-grain baking.

All-Purpose Flour (Plain Flour)

- Protein Content: 9.5–11.7 percent
- Best Uses: most everyday baking

All-purpose flour, also sometimes seen labeled as "plain flour," is a white flour produced in both bleached and unbleached varieties. It can be used for a wide variety of baked goods as it has a moderate protein content, so it will produce a moderate gluten structure.

Bread Flour

- Protein Content: 12–14.5 percent
- Best Uses: yeast bread

Bread flour is a white flour made from a wheat variety with a higher protein content than the wheat used to make all-purpose flour. Therefore, bread flour produces a stronger gluten structure in baked goods. Most bread flour is sold as unbleached flour. It is best used for baked goods where a chewy texture is desirable, such as yeast bread.

Cake Flour

- Protein Content: 6.5–8 percent
- Best Uses: cakes and delicate pastries

Cake flour is a very finely milled white flour made from wheat that has less protein than other wheat varieties. Traditionally, cake flour is also very heavily bleached (though unbleached versions do exist), which makes it softer and produces a flour that is slightly acidic. This imparts a subtle flavor that can be very desirable in some cakes. As its name suggests, cake flour is best used for cakes and delicate pastries.

Self-Rising Flour

- Protein Content: 8.5–11 percent
- Best Uses: quick breads such as biscuits, muffins, pancakes, and scones

Self-rising flour is a variety of white flour that has salt and baking powder already combined into it. This flour is traditionally used for quick breads such as biscuits, scones, and muffins, as it combines three of the most common ingredients in these recipes into one.

The name "self-rising" unfortunately has led to a common misconception that this flour can be used in place of yeast in a recipe. This is not true. Yeast and baking powder function very differently, as we will discuss in the leavening section.

Note: The UK has a similar flour called "self-raising flour." This flour is a combination of flour with only baking powder and no salt. The ratio of baking powder to flour is also higher in self-raising flour than in self-rising flour.

Whole Wheat Flour

- Protein Content: 12–14 percent
- Best Uses: substituted for a small portion of white flour in a recipe to add flavor and nutrition, or in whole-grain breads

Whole wheat flour is milled from the entire wheat grain. It has a coarser texture than white flour, but also has more flavor and nutrients. While whole wheat flours do tend to have a higher protein content than all-purpose flour, it is more difficult to create a strong gluten structure with them. For this reason, whole wheat flour is usually used in combination with white flour.

A variety of whole wheat flour, known as white whole wheat flour, is also becoming more available to consumers. This flour is still 100 percent whole wheat flour. However, it is milled from a variety of wheat that is whiter in color and milder in flavor than the variety used to make traditional whole wheat flour, which some people prefer.

Note: Whole wheat flour tends to go rancid quicker than white flour because of the natural oils present in the bran and the germ. I recommend storing whole wheat flour in the freezer to extend its shelf life.

Fats

Fat is an essential part of what makes baked goods tender and moist, but it also plays some more scientific roles in how baked goods rise.

The Function of Fats in Baking

- **Richness, Flavor, and Moisture:** The first role of fat in baking is to add richness, flavor, and moisture to baked goods. Baked goods with a lot of fat tend to taste better. Plain and simple.
- **Creates Tenderness:** Fat is a powerful tenderizer in baking. It creates a barrier between the proteins in flour and moisture, slowing down gluten development. Furthermore, fat actually works to shorten gluten strands. This is where the name for vegetable fat "shortening" came from.
- **Helps with Leavening:** Fat also plays an important role in helping baked goods to rise. When solid fat is creamed with sugar, a web of air is trapped between the two ingredients, which leavens baked goods. Additionally, butter contains some water that evaporates when baked, creating steam, lifting baked goods.

Types of Fat

There are two categories of fats used in baking: liquid fats and solid fats. Solid fats can always be melted into liquid fat form; however, they do resolidify when cooled, so they function slightly differently than true liquid fats.

Butter

Butter is the most common type of solid fat used in baking because it adds great flavor to baked goods. Butter has a fat content of around 80–83 percent, the rest being water, which makes it great for assisting with leavening. Another benefit of baking with butter is that its melting point is 90°–95°F/32–35°C, which means it literally melts in your mouth.

It is also important to note that not all butter is created equal. Most American-style butter has a fat content on the lower end of the scale, around 80 percent, while European-style butter is usually on the higher end, around 82–83 percent fat. If you are making something where butter is the star of the show and you want a very rich flavor, it might be worth splurging on European-style butter for the extra fat it contains.

 Note: Keep in mind that whipped buttery spreads and margarines that come in tubs are not a substitute for real butter in baking. These spreads have been aerated and can contain as little as 35 percent fat, which can drastically alter your final results.

Salted vs. Unsalted Butter

The only difference between salted and unsalted butter is the addition of salt in salted butter. I prefer to use unsalted butter in my baking because I like to control the amount of salt that I put into my baked goods. I typically reserve salted butter for spreading on toast and for sauteing vegetables.

All recipes in this book are written and tested with unsalted butter. If you only have salted butter on hand, you can reduce the salt by ¼ teaspoon per 113 grams (½ cup, 1 stick) of butter used in the recipe.

Vegetable Shortening

Vegetable shortening is a hydrogenated fat made from vegetable oils. Shortening contains 100 percent fat, which means it creates baked goods that are more tender than those made with butter. It also can prevent pastries, like pie crusts, from shrinking because of the lack of water evaporating out of it and its higher melting point.

Vegetable shortening has a melting point around 118°F/48°C. Due to this, baked goods made with shortening tend to not spread out as much. However, the downside is that it can leave a film in your mouth due to the fat not melting at body temperature.

Lard

Lard is a solid fat that has been rendered from a pig. It was widely used until the mid-twentieth century, when vegetable shortening was developed and lard was advertised as a less healthy option. Lard is also 100 percent fat, with a melting point around 113°F/45°C, so it functions similarly to shortening.

Leaf lard is a snowy white form of lard that is extremely mild in flavor, which makes it desirable for baking. Lard works beautifully in savory baked goods, like biscuits that will be served with sausage gravy, or in pastry for a savory pie.

Oils (Liquid Fats)

Liquid fats are all of the cooking oils. For most baking, you want to use neutral-flavored oil like canola oil, vegetable oil, safflower oil, or grapeseed oil. Olive oil is not desirable for baking unless it is specifically called for, because it is very flavorful and can be off-putting in baked goods.

All oils function the same in baking, as they are all 100 percent fat. Baked goods made with oil tend to be more tender and moist than baked goods made with solid fats because oils do not solidify once cooled.

Substituting Solid and Liquid Fats

Liquid fats should not be substituted in place of solid fat unless the recipe states that either can be used. The function of solid fats within specific mixing methods cannot be replicated with liquid fats.

However, solid fats can generally be substituted for liquid fats by melting them and allowing them to cool slightly before mixing. It should be noted, though, that the final texture will be different, as the solid fat will resolidify once cooled.

Sugar

Sugar's most prominent function in baking is to sweeten baked goods. However, it actually plays many roles in baking regarding the structure, texture, and color of baked goods as well.

 Note: Liquid sweeteners, such as honey or maple syrup, function differently than solid sugar. These are reviewed in the "miscellaneous ingredients" section.

Sugar's Role in Baking

- **Sweetens and Flavors:** While granulated sugar is fairly neutral in flavor, other varieties of sugar, such as brown sugar, add more depth of flavor in addition to the sweetness.
- **Encourages Browning:** Because of the way sugar caramelizes when heated, it also promotes the browning of baked goods. Baked goods with higher sugar ratios will brown more readily than baked goods with little to no sugar.
- **Keeps Baked Goods Moist:** Sugar is hygroscopic, meaning that it grabs and holds onto moisture. Because of this, baked goods made with sugar do not stale as quickly as baked goods made without sugar.
- **Acts as a Tenderizer:** Because sugar grabs and holds onto moisture, it leaves less readily available for the flour to absorb, slowing gluten development. Additionally, it keeps baked goods tender for a longer period of time.
- **Acts as a Leavening Agent:** When sugar is creamed with butter, or whipped with eggs, it forces a web of air to get trapped between the ingredients. This web of air lightens and helps to leaven baked goods.

Types of Sugar

Granulated Sugar (White Sugar)

Granulated sugar is a refined sugar that is white in color and is one of the most common sugars used in baking. It is slightly coarse, but still a fairly fine grain, and is neutral in flavor.

Caster Sugar (Superfine Sugar)

Caster sugar, also known as superfine sugar, is more common outside of the US. It is white sugar that is more finely ground than granulated sugar, but not as finely as powdered sugar. Castor sugar can be used as a 1:1 substitute by weight for granulated sugar. If you have a recipe that calls for superfine sugar and you only have granulated sugar available, place it in a food processor and pulse for 10 seconds.

Brown Sugar (Light & Dark)

Brown sugar is granulated sugar that has molasses added to it. Light brown sugar has a small amount of molasses, while dark brown sugar has larger amounts of molasses added. Molasses adds caramel notes to baked goods and keeps them very moist and chewy. Molasses is also acidic in nature, which means that brown sugar can be used in recipes with baking soda to activate its chemical reaction (we will address this more in depth in the leavening section). Light and dark brown sugar are typically interchangeable in baking, according to your preference for flavor. I typically use dark brown sugar because I like the rich flavor it imparts.

Powdered Sugar (Confectioner's Sugar, Icing Sugar, 10X Sugar)

Powdered sugar, which you might also see labeled as confectioner's sugar, icing sugar, or 10x sugar, is a very finely ground white sugar. It is also mixed with an anticaking agent, such as cornstarch, to prevent clumping. Powdered sugar dissolves extremely quickly into baked goods, and because of the starch, it can create a very tender final product.

Turbinado Sugar (Raw Sugar)

Turbinado sugar, also known as raw sugar, is a type of sugar that has been minimally processed. The texture is very coarse, and it works well in baking as a topping for muffins, scones, or other pastries, to add a crunchy texture.

Eggs

While egg is only one ingredient, it deserves a whole section to itself because of the many roles it plays in baking. Eggs are utilized in three forms in baking: whole eggs, egg whites, and egg yolks. Each form has a different function, so let's review each.

White Eggs vs. Brown Eggs

The only difference between brown eggs and white eggs is the breed of chicken they come from. There is no difference nutritionally between the two.

Brown eggs have long been associated with the eggs that are sold as organic and free-range, and therefore there is a misconception that brown eggs are inherently healthier. However, white eggs can just as easily carry these labels.

Egg Sizing

Eggs are sold in a variety of sizes according to their weight: small, medium, large, extra-large, and jumbo. Large eggs are the most common size used for baking, and what all recipes in this book are written and tested with.

With farm-fresh eggs, the sizes can vary greatly in a carton. This likely won't cause many issues if your recipe only calls for one or two eggs, as the size difference between a medium and a large egg isn't substantial. However, this can become incrementally more crucial if you are baking on a larger scale. A large egg without the shell weighs about 50 grams (32 grams white, 18 grams yolk). If you have eggs of varying sizes, it can be helpful to weigh them for your recipes, especially if the recipe calls for a large number of eggs.

 Tip: If you need part of an egg for a recipe, whisk the yolk and the white together and then weigh out the amount you need.

The Function of Whole Eggs in Baking

The makeup of a whole egg includes a good amount of water, as well as protein and fat. These three things work together to perform several functions.

- **Binder:** Whole eggs work to bind baked goods together because of the protein content and because egg yolks gel as they heat up. This adds structure and strength to baked goods.
- **Leavening:** Whole eggs contain quite a bit of water. As the water evaporates off the egg in the oven, it helps leaven baked goods.
- **Adds Flavor and Color:** Whole eggs add flavor, color, and richness.
- **Tenderness:** The fat in whole eggs adds tenderness and moisture.

How to Separate an Egg

When separating eggs, it is very important that no egg yolk gets into the egg white. Egg whites will not foam properly if any fat is present in them.

The best way to separate an egg is with clean hands and three bowls. One bowl is for cracking the egg into, one bowl is for the yolks, and the other is for the whites. This ensures that you don't get any yolk into the already separated whites. If any yolk gets into the bowl of whites, you will have to start over.

1. Crack the egg into one bowl.
2. Pick the egg up with clean hands and let the white fall off the yolk.
3. Put the yolk in one bowl and the white in another bowl.

The Function of Egg Whites in Baking

The egg white is about two-thirds of the total volume of the egg and is made up of mostly water and some protein. The egg white does not contain any fat, so it performs a very different role than the egg yolk.

- **Lighten and Leaven:** Egg whites can be whipped to create an egg white foam, which helps to lighten and leaven baked goods. Egg white foam is often folded into cake batters to create an incredibly light texture. Egg whites are also often whipped into a foam with the addition of sugar for meringue, which is its own pastry component (page 217).

- **Create Crispness:** Because of the water present in egg whites and the absence of fat, they can tend to have a drying effect on baked goods and can help to create a crispy texture.

The Function of Egg Yolks in Baking

Egg yolk makes up the other one-third of the whole egg and contains a high percentage of fat as well as some protein and water. When a recipe calls for only yolks, it is typically because the fat content, as well as the yolk's ability to emulsify, is desired.

- **Add Richness:** Egg yolks add richness to baked goods due to the fat content.
- **Emulsify:** Egg yolks are great emulsifiers, meaning they work to combine water-based liquid and fats into one cohesive mixture. This function helps create a smoother and more homogeneous batter or dough.
- **Enhance Color:** Egg yolks add flavor and color.
- **Thicken Mixtures:** Egg yolks also thicken mixtures when they are heated because the proteins begin to gel. You will see this very clearly when making custards like pastry cream (page 207) or fruit curd (page 211).

Leavening Agents

Leavening refers to the gases that are trapped in a baked good during baking. There are numerous ways baked goods are leavened. Whatever method is utilized, leavening is an extremely important part of baking.

There are three main categories of leavening utilized in baking:

- Chemical leavening (baking powder and baking soda)
- Biological leavening (yeast)
- Physical leavening (air and steam)

Chemical Leavening

Both baking soda and baking powder are forms of chemical leavening. When they are added to a baked good, a chemical reaction occurs that produces carbon dioxide. This gas gets trapped in the structure of the baked good as it bakes and leavens it. There are two points at which chemical leavening reacts: once when it is put in contact with an acidic ingredient, and again when heated.

Baking Soda

Baking soda, also known as sodium bicarbonate, is alkaline on the pH scale. Therefore, it needs an acidic ingredient in the recipe to interact with. If a recipe does not contain an acidic ingredient, the baking soda will not begin creating carbon dioxide gas until well into the baking process, at which point it is usually too late to fully leaven the baked good. Baking soda will also leave a bitter or metallic aftertaste if it does not interact with an acidic ingredient.

Baking soda is about four times more powerful by volume than baking powder. You might notice that the amount of baking soda called for in a recipe is usually quite a bit less than the amount of baking powder.

Common Acidic Ingredients for Baking Soda to Interact with:

- Brown sugar
- Buttermilk
- Sour cream and yogurt
- Cream of tartar
- Natural cocoa powder (not Dutch-processed)
- Melted chocolate (solid chocolate, like chocolate chips, will not interact with baking soda)
- Molasses
- Honey
- Lemon juice
- Vinegar

Baking Powder

Baking powder is a complete leavening system, meaning that it is a combination of baking soda and an acidic ingredient. Baking powder does not need an additional acidic ingredient in the recipe in order to properly leaven baked goods and will begin reacting as soon as it is hydrated.

Most baking powder is also "double-acting." This means that it actually contains two acidic ingredients; one that will activate when hydrated, and a second that will activate when heated, creating a second burst of activity in the oven.

Why Some Recipes Use Both Baking Soda and Baking Powder:

Recipes that call for both baking soda and baking powder usually contain some acid that needs to be neutralized by the baking soda, but likely not enough to do the amount of leavening that is desired. Therefore, baking powder will pick up the slack.

Biological Leavening

Yeast

Yeast is known as a biological leavening agent because it is a living organism—a fungus! Yeast feeds on sugars and starches present in the dough and produces carbon dioxide gas and alcohol. This process is called fermentation, and it is what makes yeast dough rise. This topic is covered more in depth in Chapter 9.

Physical Leavening

Air

Air is a type of physical leavening that is used frequently in baking. The most common instance is when butter and sugar are beaten together. This process is called "creaming," and it forces air to get trapped in a web of sugar and fat, adding volume to baked goods.

Air is also used when whipping eggs or cream into a foam. This process traps little air pockets in the substance which lightens and leavens.

Focaccia (page 237), leavened with yeast

Steam

Steam is another powerful type of physical leavening. Certain ingredients, such as butter, eggs, and milk, contain water that will evaporate in the oven, creating steam. While this may not sound as exciting as the chemical and biological reactions of other leavening agents, when water evaporates, it *increases in volume by 1,500 times!* This means steam can create a great deal of volume in baked goods.

Dairy Products

Dairy products like milk, sour cream, and buttermilk are used mostly for adding moisture, flavor, and richness to baked goods. However, there are some dairy products that are acidic in nature, and therefore play a more scientific role in the way they interact with the other ingredients.

Milk

The main function of milk is to add moisture and richness to baked goods. The higher the fat content of the milk you are using, the richer and more tender your baked good will be.

In general, if your recipe calls for low-fat, 1 percent, or 2 percent milk, you can substitute it with what you have on hand, or even with dairy-free milk, with little consequence to the final baked good. If the recipe calls for higher-fat milk, like whole milk, half and half, or cream, you need to be more careful in making any substitution.

Cream

Heavy cream, whipping cream, and double cream are unique in that they have a fat content of at least 30 percent, which allows them to be whipped into a foam. These products are often used for moisture and richness in baking. However, they can also be used to help lighten and aerate when folded into a filling or something like a mousse.

Buttermilk, Sour Cream, and Yogurt

Buttermilk, sour cream, and yogurt are all cultured dairy products, which means they are acidic in nature. These products are used frequently in baking to activate baking soda, in addition to adding moisture and flavor to baked goods.

Other Important Ingredients

Now that we have covered all of the most important categories of ingredients, I want to quickly review a few other key ingredients that are important to note.

Salt

Salt is one of the most underrated ingredients in baking. Baked goods made without salt will taste flat and boring. Salt enhances and balances flavors, especially sweetness. The proper amount of salt can take a mediocre recipe and make it outstanding.

I personally prefer to use kosher salt in all of my cooking and baking, with the exception of cakes, where I prefer to use fine sea salt. Kosher salt has a coarser grain, and I like the way it gives little flecks of saltiness throughout the baked good, rather than blending in completely. For cakes, I find it more necessary for the salt to be more evenly dispersed. However, this is completely a personal preference, and you can use fine sea salt for all of your baking if you prefer.

 Note: If you only have table salt on hand, you will want to reduce the amount by half for all recipes in this book, as it is much saltier by volume than other salts.

Cocoa Powder

Cocoa powder for baking is sold in two main forms: natural cocoa powder and Dutch-processed (also known as alkalized) cocoa powder. Both types serve the purpose of adding chocolate flavor and color to baked goods, but they do differ slightly in flavor and function.

Natural cocoa powder is acidic and is often used as the acidic ingredient needed in recipes that contain baking soda. It is lighter in color when compared to Dutched cocoa powder; however, it typically has a richer chocolate flavor that tastes brighter and fruitier than Dutched cocoa.

Dutch-processed cocoa powder has gone through a chemical process to neutralize the cocoa's natural acidity. Dutched cocoa can give the appearance of a richer chocolate flavor because it is darker in color; however, the flavor is a bit milder than natural cocoa powder but is also more complex.

If a recipe has been written properly, it should specify which cocoa to use, or if either can be used. It is important to note that not all cocoa powders are clearly labeled with natural or Dutched identifiers. To identify your cocoa, look at the ingredients label. Dutch-processed cocoa powder will list something like "Dutched cocoa powder," "cocoa powder processed with alkali," or "alkalized cocoa powder."

Extracts and Spices

In baking, ingredients like vanilla and almond extract, and spices like cinnamon, only serve the purpose of flavoring baked goods. They do not contribute to the structure or the chemistry of the recipe's formula. Spices and extracts are a fun way to play with flavors without altering the final texture of your baked goods.

Spices lose their potency over time. Some say that ground spices should be replaced every three months. This isn't very practical for most. My general rule of thumb is to use spices within a year of purchase for the best flavor.

Liquid Sweeteners

Liquid sweeteners, like honey, maple syrup, corn syrup, and molasses, function quite differently in baking than solid sugars. There isn't an easy way to substitute liquid sweeteners for sugar in a recipe because of this. It is best to use recipes that are written for utilizing liquid sweeteners if you prefer to use them over sugar.

Ingredient Substitutions

One of the most frequently asked questions I get is how to substitute ingredients. As a general rule of thumb, the best approach is to find a recipe that utilizes the specific ingredients you have available to you. As you now know, baking is a science, and making any changes can affect the final result of your baked goods. Always proceed with caution when making substitutions.

This is not to say that you can't ever make substitutions! Here are a few common scenarios where substitutions can easily be made with success.

Making a Recipe Gluten-Free

- **Substitution:** All-Purpose Gluten-Free Baking Blend, 1:1 Ratio
- **Best Used For:** Quick breads (muffins, batter breads, pancakes, waffles), cookies, and bars
- **Not Recommended For:** Yeast breads, delicate cakes, or pastries

The easiest way to make a recipe gluten-free is to utilize an all-purpose gluten-free baking blend. These blends have been specifically formulated with a combination of flours, starches, and gums to function in a similar way to gluten.

Utilizing a gluten-free baking blend typically works best for recipes like quick breads, cookies, and bars. Some cakes and pastries can work well with gluten-free baking blends, but it really depends on the recipe. For delicate baked goods, I recommend finding a gluten-free recipe that has been specifically developed that way.

Yeast breads are also incredibly difficult to make gluten-free, as gluten plays such an important role in trapping the gases from the yeast. I do not recommend trying to substitute gluten-free flour into a traditional bread recipe; rather, seek out a trusted gluten-free source for a well-tested recipe.

Making a Recipe Egg-Free

- **Substitution Options:**

  - *Commercial Egg Replacer:* Follow package recommendations for amounts to use.
  - *Flax or Chia "Egg":* Combine 7 grams (1 tablespoon) chia seeds or ground flax with 43 grams (3 tablespoons) water for every egg you are substituting. Let sit for 5 minutes, until thickened, before using.
  - *Applesauce or Mashed Banana:* Use 65 grams (¼ cup) applesauce or mashed banana for every egg you are substituting.

- **Best Used For:** Quick breads (muffins, batter breads, pancakes, waffles), cookies, and bars
- **Not Recommended For:** Yeast breads, cakes, or pastries

Eggs play many different roles in baking, so you do want to be cautious when substituting them. I encourage you to ask yourself, "What function is the egg playing in this specific recipe?" If the egg's role is simply to add moisture and to bind, then substitutions can work well. Quick breads, cookies, and bars are typically fairly safe for making egg substitutions.

However, if the answer is to lighten and leaven, like in a cake where you are whipping air into egg whites, then you likely will want to find a different recipe that is specifically developed as egg-free.

Making a Recipe Dairy-Free

- **Substitution:** Dairy-Free Milk and Vegan Butter or Shortening, 1:1 Ratio
- **Best Used For:** Quick breads, cookies, bars, pastries, cakes
- **Not Recommended For:** Cheesecakes

Most baking recipes can easily be made dairy-free by swapping in non-dairy milk in place of dairy milk and vegan butter or shortening in place of butter. There are a few instances where this might not work well. However, keep in mind that these substitutions can definitely alter the flavor of your baked goods, depending on the quantity in the recipe.

Recipes where dairy is the main ingredient also do not typically work well for direct substitutions, such as cheesecake. If dairy is the star of the show, I highly recommend finding a recipe that has been specifically developed to be dairy-free.

Substituting Buttermilk

- **Substitution Options:**

    - *Yogurt or Sour Cream + Water:* Combine 57 grams (¼ cup) water with 180 grams (¾ cup) plain yogurt or sour cream to replace 240 grams (1 cup) of buttermilk
    - *Powdered Buttermilk:* Mix with water according to package instructions
    - *Kefir (drinkable yogurt):* 1:1 ratio
    - *Milk + White Vinegar or Lemon Juice:* Combine 28 grams (2 tablespoons) white vinegar or lemon juice with 200 grams (1 cup minus 2 tablespoons) milk of choice for every cup of buttermilk. Let stand 5–10 minutes before using.

- **Best Used For:** Any recipe that calls for buttermilk

Buttermilk's role in a recipe is typically to activate the baking soda, as well as to provide some flavor and tenderness, with its acidic nature. When substituting, these functions are important to keep in mind.

My favorite buttermilk substitute is plain yogurt or sour cream mixed with a bit of water. This substitute gets closest to the flavor and texture of real buttermilk, and I find it gives the best results. You can also purchase powdered buttermilk that can be mixed with water. This is a great option to keep in your pantry for last-minute needs.

The most common substitution you may have heard of is mixing milk with white vinegar or lemon juice. This is my least favorite option. Buttermilk is a cultured product, and therefore has a thick texture. This substitution will be significantly thinner than real buttermilk. If using this substitution, I recommend holding a little bit back when first mixing it into your dough or batter, as you might not need all of it. Once mixed, you can decide to add the rest if needed.

Substituting Cake Flour

- **Substitution:** 15 grams (2 tablespoons) cornstarch or arrowroot + 105 grams (¾ cup plus 2 tablespoons) all-purpose flour for every 115 grams (1 cup) of cake flour you are substituting. Sift together three times to aerate.
- **Best Used For:** Any recipe that calls for cake flour.

Technically, you can substitute plain all-purpose flour for cake flour at a 1:1 ratio by weight (cake flour does weigh less per cup than all-purpose flour). However, your cake will definitely have a denser texture and will not be as fluffy.

The best substitution for cake flour is to combine some all-purpose flour with some cornstarch or arrowroot and sift it together several times, as above. This combination will give your cake the closest texture to using the real thing.

Ingredient Temperatures

Ingredient temperature is another one of the major factors that can affect the final result of your baked goods. If a recipe is written properly, it should specify when ingredients should be at room temperature or when they should be cold. However, there are a few rules of thumb to keep in mind in case you come across a recipe that doesn't specifically indicate ingredient temperatures.

Which Ingredients Matter?

When we are discussing ingredient temperatures for baking, we are talking about ingredients that are typically kept in the refrigerator. This includes things like butter, milk, cream, cream cheese, eggs, and sour cream. Dry ingredients like sugar and flour should always be used at room temperature.

When Ingredients Should be Cold

As a general rule of thumb, you want to use cold ingredients for any kind of baked good with a flaky final texture. Examples of this are pie crusts, biscuits, scones, and puff pastry.

For all of these examples, it is important that the fat remain solid before the baked good goes into the oven. The solid fat will melt in the oven, creating little pockets of flakiness. For these recipes, you also want to make sure your butter, eggs, cream, and/or milk are cold before making the dough. We will review this concept more in depth in Chapter 5.

Whipping cream into a foam for whipped cream is another specific instance where it is extremely important for the ingredient to be cold. Cream will not thicken and trap a web of air if it is not cold. The colder it is, the quicker it will thicken.

When Ingredients Should be Room Temperature

If you are making something with a cohesive final texture, as opposed to a flaky final texture, in general, your ingredients should be at room temperature. Ingredients are more readily absorbed into batters and doughs when they are at room temperature.

Butter and sugar also cannot be properly creamed together if the butter is too cold or too warm. Either the creamed mixture won't be able to form, or the mixture could break, which will likely result in an undesirable final texture. Furthermore, if the other ingredients you add into your creamed mixture, like eggs or milk, are cold or too warm, they can also break the creamed mixture.

Whipping egg whites into a foam is another instance where it is important for ingredients to be at room temperature. Egg whites will not whip up to their highest volume if they are cold.

What Does "Room Temperature" Mean?

In baking, room temperature is assumed to be somewhere around 68–72°F (20–22°C). This is the temperature at which butter is soft, but not melting or greasy-looking. Once butter gets to the point where it starts looking greasy or is starting to melt, you should pop it back into the refrigerator for a few minutes before using it to cream with sugar.

How to Quickly Bring Your Ingredients to Room Temperature

Depending on the temperature of your kitchen, it can take anywhere from 30 minutes to an hour for most ingredients to come to room temperature. My kitchen sits around 70°F (21°C), and I typically give my ingredients at least 45 minutes. But if your kitchen is warmer or cooler, you will want to adjust the length of time accordingly.

While it is typically ideal to pull your ingredients out with enough time for them to naturally come to room temperature, this isn't always possible. We've all had a last-minute craving for chocolate chip cookies!

To quickly soften butter, cut it into small pieces and spread them out! Small pieces will come to room temperature much quicker than one larger mass. If you're really in a hurry, you can microwave it in 5-second bursts at 50 percent power. But watch it closely! You don't want it to start melting. It should be soft, but still cool to the touch. This technique also works well for cream cheese.

To bring eggs to room temperature, place them in a bowl of warm, not hot, water before cracking. This will take the chill off in about 5–10 minutes.

To bring milk, buttermilk, cream, sour cream, or yogurt to room temperature, I microwave it in 10-second bursts at 50 percent power, stirring in between bursts.

2

Essential Baking Equipment

To get started baking, there are a few pieces of equipment that are essential and will set you up for success. This book does not call for many specialty pieces of equipment, and most items can be used for a wide variety of bakes.

Measuring Tools

I strongly encourage you to begin measuring by weight. We will discuss this in more depth in Chapter 4, but a digital scale is highly recommended. A set of measuring spoons is also very necessary for measuring things that are too small to be weighed.

If you do want to measure by volume, you will need both dry and liquid measuring cups. While dry and liquid measuring cups measure the same amount by volume, they function differently. Dry measuring cups have a blunt edge that allows dry ingredients to be leveled off. Due to surface tension, liquids would need to look like they are overflowing the dry measuring cup in order to have an accurate measurement.

In contrast, liquid measuring cups have a pour spout with a variety of volume markings on the side. For liquids, you can get down to eye level to see that your measurement is accurate. However, dry ingredients cannot be accurately leveled in a liquid measuring cup. Even if you do measure by weight, measuring cups can be helpful to have on hand for certain circumstances.

- Digital scale
- Measuring spoons
- Dry measuring cups and liquid measuring cups

 Note: All volume measurements in this book are based on a "Legal US Cup," which is 240 milliliters (8 fluid ounces). However, be aware that many places outside the US have metric measuring cups that are based on 250 milliliters per cup.

Mixing Tools

A whisk and a silicone spatula are by far the most-used mixing tools in baking. I recommend having several of each in your kitchen. You will also need either an electric hand mixer or a stand mixer for several recipes in this book. It is very difficult to cream butter and sugar together without an electric mixer. However, it does not need to be fancy. I have had my $25 handheld mixer for over ten years, and it gets the job done.

- Mixing bowls
- Whisk
- Silicone spatula
- Mixing spoons
- Hand mixer or stand mixer
- Sifter

Baking Pans

I am a big advocate for investing in sturdy, rimmed half-sheet pans instead of flimsy cookie sheets for baking. If you already have cookie sheets, they will work just fine for you. But if you are in the market for new pans, seek out some good quality half-sheet pans. They will last your lifetime. I recommend having at least two in your kitchen.

There are also a few other baking pans that will be utilized in this book and are essential in a baker's kitchen. For most baking instances, I prefer metal pans as it is the best conductor of heat. Glass or ceramic pans are best for items that have long bake times, like pies or casseroles.

- 18 x 13-inch (46 x 33-cm) rimmed baking sheets (a.k.a. half-sheet pan)
- 9 x 13-inch (23 x 33-cm) baking pan (preferably metal)
- 8-inch (20-cm) square baking pan (preferably metal)
- Two 12-cup standard-size muffin/cupcake tins
- 8.5 x 4.5-inch (22 x 11-cm) loaf pan (preferably metal)
- 9-inch (23-cm) deep dish pie plate
- *Three 8-inch (20-cm) or two 9-inch (23-cm) circular cake pans
- *Tube pan
- *12-cup Bundt cake pan
- *9-inch (23-cm) spring form pan

*indicates pans that are optional but helpful to have

Miscellaneous Tools

There are a few more miscellaneous tools that you will find to be essential in your kitchen. One tool that I didn't start using until culinary school is a bench knife. Now it is one of my most-used kitchen tools for things like cutting dough, transferring items to baking sheets, smoothing icing on a cake, and cleaning scraps of dough off my counter.

- Oven thermometer
- Rolling pin
- Cooling rack
- Pastry blender
- *Bench knife
- *Bowl scraper

- *Pastry brush
- *Offset spatula
- *Portioning scoops (a.k.a. dishers): 1 oz./30 ml for cookies, 1.5 oz./45 ml for cupcakes, muffins, and ice cream
- *Muffin/cupcake liners
- Parchment paper or silicone baking mats
- Plastic wrap
- *Candy thermometer
- *Fine mesh sieve

*indicates tools that are optional but helpful to have

Oven Thermometer

One of the most helpful kitchen tools a baker can rely on for better baking is an oven thermometer. It is very common for ovens to either heat hotter or cooler, sometimes by as much as 50°F/10°C, than the temperature they are set at. It is also common for the oven indicator to alert that the oven is fully preheated before it truly is. Ovens not being heated to the proper temperature can cause endless issues with your baked goods!

To use an oven thermometer, place it in the center of the oven and preheat it to 350°F/175°C for 20 full minutes with the door closed. Then check the reading on the thermometer. You can use this information to adjust up or down where you set the oven temperature, or better yet, have your oven serviced to get it calibrated to the proper settings.

Bundt Pan

Tube Pan

Pastry Blender

Offset Spatula

Liquid Measuring Cup

Dry Measuring Cups

Disher/Scoop

Bowl Scraper

Oven Thermometer

Measuring Spoons

Bench Knife

Candy Thermometer

Fine Mesh Sie

Digital Scale

TAYLOR

3

Common Baking Techniques and Terminology

When I first started baking, I would often read a recipe that included terminology I did not understand. It was discouraging and frustrating to sort through. And even when I learned what something like "cut in the butter" meant, I wouldn't understand the purpose. This chapter will be a resource for you to reference all of the most common baking terminology and techniques, as well as the purpose of each.

Batter

- **Definition**: A batter is an unbaked mixture that is thin enough to pour or scoop but cannot be rolled out like a dough.
- **Baked Goods That Are Made with Batters**: Muffins, quick loaf breads (a.k.a. batter breads), cakes, cupcakes, and brownies.
- **Tips for Making a Batter**: Take care to not overmix batters, or too much gluten will develop, creating a tough baked good. Mix only until all of the ingredients are incorporated.

Blind Baking

- **Definition**: Blind baking is when a crust for a pie or tart is baked before the filling is added. This is done when the filling does not need to be baked, or if the filling does not need to bake as long as the crust does.
- **Baked Goods That Utilize Blind Baking**: Most tarts and pies with no-bake fillings or custard fillings.
- **Tips for Blind Baking**: Make sure you blind-bake with pie weights in your crust to prevent it from shrinking or puffing up too much in the oven. We will review this more in Chapter 8.

Bulk-Ferment

- **Definition**: Bulk-ferment refers to the stage of a yeast dough after it has been mixed and kneaded but before it has been shaped. You might also hear this called "the first rise."
- **Tips for Bulk Fermentation**: Bulk fermentation is complete after the dough has at least doubled in size and, if you press a finger into it, the indentation remains.

Caramelize

- **Definition**: Caramelization refers to the change sugar goes through when it is heated and allowed to brown. Caramelization creates a more complex flavor and becomes much less sweet than pure sugar.
- **When It's Used**: Sugar is caramelized for making sugar decorations, as well as for dessert sauces and candies.
- **Tips for Caramelizing Sugar**: Never walk away from sugar while it is caramelizing. Once the sugar begins browning, it moves very quickly. The darker the color of the sugar, the more bitter it becomes.

Creaming

- **Definition**: When a baking recipe instructs you to "cream together," it is referring to when solid fat is beaten together with sugar. The process of beating the two together forms a web of air between the fat and sugar, which lightens and leavens baked goods.
- **When It's Used**: When making cookies, buttercream frosting, and butter-based cakes.
- **Tips for Creaming**: Butter needs to be at a cool room temperature (around 68–72°F / 20–22°C) to be properly creamed with sugar. If it is too cold or too warm, the mixture will separate and will not hold the web of air.

Cut In

- **Definition**: Cutting in fat refers to when pieces of solid fat are worked into flour until it is starts to coat the flour and small pieces of fat are distributed throughout. This process is typically executed by utilizing a tool called a pastry blender.
- **When It's Used**: Fat is cut into flour when making baked goods that result in a very flaky final product, such as biscuits, scones, and pie crusts. The process of coating the flour in fat keeps the proteins from forming too much gluten. This process also disperses small pieces of solid fat throughout the dough which will melt in the oven, creating pockets of steam that create a flaky baked good.
- **Tips for Cutting in Fat**: When a recipe calls for fat to be cut into flour, it is essential that the fat be very cold. This ensures the fat stays solid until it bakes, which will create pockets of flakiness.

Crimp

- **Definition**: Crimping refers to folding the edges of dough in a decorative way. It also serves to seal two pieces of dough together to prevent the filling from leaking.
- **When It's Used**: To finish the edges of pie crusts or tarts, or when sealing a hand pie or turnover.
- **Tips for Crimping**: Dip your fingers or crimping tool in flour to prevent them from sticking to the dough while crimping.

Crumb

- **Definition**: Crumb refers to the holes inside your baked good and how small, large, even, or uneven they are. For instance, a delicate cake should have a tight yet even crumb when you cut into it, while a flaky biscuit should have a more open crumb that is uneven.
- **Why Assessing Crumb Matters**: The crumb is a clear indication of the texture of your final baked good, and whether the technique was executed properly. Assessing the crumb can help identify what might have gone wrong.

Dock

- **Definition**: When a pie or tart crust is pricked all over with a fork to allow steam to exit while the crust is baking. This helps prevent the crust from puffing up and shrinking.
- **When It's Used**: Docking is typically used when blind baking a pie or tart crust.
- **Tips for Docking**: Prick the crust all around the bottom as well as up the sides of the pan.

Dough

- **Definition**: A dough is a thick unbaked mixture (thicker than a batter) that can be rolled out or shaped by hand.
- **Baked Goods Made with Doughs**: Yeast breads, biscuits, scones, cookies, pie, and tart crusts.
- **Tips for Working with Dough**: If you are handling a dough that is too sticky, you can always lightly flour your countertop. However, be cautious not to use too much flour when shaping yeast bread dough, as you want the dough to naturally stick to itself to help build tension and hold its shape.

Emulsion

- **Definition**: An emulsion is a forced mixture of two ingredients that are normally unmixable (for instance, water and fat). When ingredients are emulsified, particles from the two substances are suspended within each other instead of quickly separating.
- **When It's Used**: Many common baking ingredients are already emulsions. Milk and butter are examples of ingredients that are already emulsified. There are also many instances in baking where it is important not to break these emulsions, such as when adding eggs into creamed butter. If the eggs are too cold or if they are added in too quickly, it can cause the butter to break, and the eggs will not emulsify into the butter.

- **Tips for Creating Emulsions**: It is important to slowly incorporate ingredients when working to create an emulsion, or when adding ingredients to an emulsion that already exists.

Ferment

- **Definition**: In baking, fermentation refers to the process of yeast feeding on sugars and starches present in yeast dough. As the yeast feeds, it produces carbon dioxide, which makes the dough rise. This process is also what develops the distinctive flavor of yeast breads.
- **Tips for Fermentation**: The speed of fermentation depends heavily on temperature. Cooler temperatures will slow down the fermentation process, while warmer temperatures will speed it up.

Folding

- **Definition**: Folding is a technique used to incorporate two mixtures together in a very delicate way. This technique serves to reduce gluten development and prevent whipped egg whites or whipped cream from deflating when being mixed into another component.
- **When It's Used**: Folding is used particularly when adding meringue or whipped cream into a batter or another ingredient, or when adding solid mix-ins into a batter to avoid overworking the gluten structure.
- **How to Properly Execute Folding**: When folding, a rubber spatula should be used. The delicate mixture should be added to the heavier mixture. Add about a quarter of the delicate ingredient into the bowl and stir it in completely to lighten the batter. Then add about half of the rest of the delicate mixture and use the spatula to cut down through the middle of two mixtures, to the bottom of the bowl, bringing the ingredients at the bottom of the bowl up. Turn the bowl 90 degrees, scrape the side of the bowl, and continue with this motion until the ingredients are incorporated.

Gluten

- **Definition**: When the proteins found in wheat flour (glutenin and gliadin) are hydrated, they bond together, forming what is referred to as gluten. As the hydrated flour is worked more, the gluten strands begin to align, becoming more and more elastic.
- **Why Gluten Development Matters**: Gluten development is what creates the main structure in traditional baked goods. In tender baked goods, such as cakes and flaky pastries, it is important to limit this process so that you don't end up with a tough baked good. For baked goods leavened with yeast, it is important to really develop the gluten structure in order for the dough to contain the gases that yeast creates over time.
- **Tips for Managing Gluten Development**: The gluten structure becomes stronger and more elastic the more a dough or batter is worked. For delicate baked goods, take care not to overmix the batter or handle the dough too much. In contrast, for bread dough, kneading the dough for an extended period of time will build a strong gluten structure, which is desirable.

Knead

- **Definition**: Kneading is the process where dough is worked and stretched to build strength and elasticity through gluten development.
- **When It's Used**: This process is most commonly used when making yeast bread.
- **Tips for Kneading**: Kneading can be done by hand or with a dough hook on a stand mixer. Dough will become more elastic and less sticky as it is kneaded, so try to avoid adding too much extra flour toward the beginning of the process. Kneading is discussed and shown in more depth in Chapter 9.

Leaven, Leavening

- **Definition**: In baking, the word leaven refers to the process of a baked good rising.
- **When It's Used**: Leavening is used in at least one form in practically every baked good.

Peaks (Soft, Medium, Stiff)

- **What Are Soft, Medium, and Stiff Peaks?**: In baking, peaks refer to the stiffness of cream or egg whites when air has been beaten into them. As cream or egg whites are whipped, more air is incorporated, and the mixture becomes thicker. To assess the peaks, stir your mixture with your beater

Baker Bettie's Better Baking Book

or whisk, then lift it out of your mixing bowl, turn it upside down, and look at the peaks of egg whites or cream coming off the mixing tool. Soft peaks barely hold their shape. Medium peaks hold shape, but the peaks curl at the tip. Stiff peaks stand straight up and do not curl over, or curl just slightly at the tip.

- **When Peaks Matter in Baking**: When whipping egg whites or cream.
- **Tips for Whipping Cream and Egg Whites**: Cream needs to be cold to hold a web of air and thicken, while egg whites whip up much quicker when they are at room temperature, or slightly warm, than when cold.

| Soft peaks | Medium peaks | Stiff peaks |

Proof or Prove

- **Definition**: Proofing refers to the final rise a yeast dough goes through after being shaped and before it is baked. Sometimes, the word "proof" is also used for the first rise the dough goes through (the bulk fermentation stage). To prevent confusion, we will only use "proof" when referring to the final rise of the shaped dough in this book and will use "bulk fermentation" for the first rise.
- **When It's Used**: When making a yeast bread or yeasted pastry.
- **Tips for Proofing**: To check whether your dough is finished proofing, gently press in on it about a half-inch with your finger. If the indentation fills in quickly (in less than a second), it needs a bit more time to rise. If it springs back slowly, it is ready to bake. If the indentation does not fill in at all, or the dough feels as though it may collapse, it has over-proofed, and the baked good will be dense after baking.

Score

- **Definition**: Scoring refers to shallow cuts made on unbaked dough. Scoring is used to control where bread dough will split, as well as to release steam from filled pastries. It can also be decorative.
- **When It's Used**: In bread making and in some filled pastries, like double-crust pies or hand pies.

- **Tips for Scoring**: When scoring bread dough or pastries, a very sharp knife, a serrated knife, or a specialty tool called a bread lame works best. This will allow you to cut the dough in clean lines and not tear it.

Sift

- **Definition**: Sifting is a process of forcing flour and other dry ingredients through a fine mesh to break up any lumps and to aerate the ingredients.
- **When It's Used**: Sifted flour is much lighter and incorporates into a batter or dough more easily. Flour and other dry ingredients should be sifted when making light and tender baked goods, such as cakes and delicate pastries. Ingredients that tend to clump, like powdered sugar and cocoa powder, should also be sifted.
- **Tips for Sifting**: If measuring by volume, ingredients should always be sifted after they are measured (unless otherwise specified by the recipe) because the ingredient will increase in volume after sifting.

Softened

- **Definition**: When a recipe calls for butter to be "softened," the butter should be at a cool room temperature, somewhere between 68–72°F/20–22°C.
- **When It's Used**: Softened butter is used when it will be creamed with sugar in a recipe. The butter needs to be softened so that it will hold a web of air after being beaten with the sugar.
- **Tips for Softening Butter**: Butter can easily be softened by being left to sit out at room temperature for 30–45 minutes. Butter will soften more quickly if it is cut up into small pieces.

Tempering

- **Definition**: Tempering is the process of slowly combining two ingredients that are at different temperatures in order to bring them to a similar temperature before mixing them completely.
- **When It's Used**: Tempering is most often used by home bakers when they need to mix eggs with a hot liquid. To avoid scrambling and cooking the eggs, you want to add a small amount of the hot liquid to the egg mixture, to gently warm it up, before slowly adding in the rest of the hot mixture. Tempering also refers to a process used in more advanced pastry applications where chocolate is heated and cooled in a way that stabilizes it.
- **Tips for Tempering**: Go slowly and take your time when tempering.

4

Essential Rules of Baking

I know you are likely ready to jump into baking, and I promise we are almost there! I have just a few more things that are very important before we get started. The rules covered in this chapter are essential for your baking success!

Measuring Properly

One of the most common mistakes made by new bakers is not measuring ingredients properly. Yes, measuring is actually a skill!

Measuring mistakes typically occur when measuring by volume, meaning using measuring cups instead of a scale. This method of measuring uses the amount of space an ingredient takes up as the measurement, instead of how much it weighs. It is very common for this to be inaccurate, depending on a variety of factors.

For instance, flour provides the main structure for most baked goods. Flour is also a powdery dry ingredient that is very easy to pack into a measuring cup. If you ask five people to measure out a cup of flour and then weigh each of them, you will likely have five different weights. Packing down the flour, not leveling properly, and scooping the flour with the measuring cup instead of spooning it into the cup, can all affect how much flour takes up a given amount of space. Additionally, not all measuring cups are completely accurate in size. This can cause many issues with your baked goods.

I highly encourage you to start measuring by weight if you do not already. I know it is common in the US to use cup measurements, and this is how I first learned to bake. However, if you start getting in the habit of using weight measurements, you will not only find it much easier, but you will have more consistency with your bakes. It also makes scaling recipes up or down based on your needs very easy! I thought measuring by weight was fussier and more difficult before I adopted it. Once I got used to it, I found it to actually be a much quicker and easier process than using measuring cups.

That said, I'm still going to review how to use both weight and volume measuring techniques. Most US recipes tend to use cup volume measurements, while recipes outside the US tend to use metric weight measurements for solid ingredients and metric volume measurements for liquids. The recipes in this book list weight measurements for ingredients first, as it is what I hope you will use. The recipes also include volume measurements (in both cups and milliliters) and have been thoroughly tested both ways. If you do choose to measure with a measuring cup, I want to make sure you know how to do it properly.

Ounces vs. Fluid Ounces

In the US, there are two different types of "ounces" that are used when measuring: Ounces, which are a weight measurement (used for solids), and fluid ounces, which are a volume measurement (used for liquids). This can cause a lot of confusion when measuring. Many people have heard that "one cup is 8 ounces." But it is important to note that this statement is referring to fluid ounces (volume) and not weight.

Where the confusion comes in is that most liquids measure the same in weight ounces as in fluid ounces. Eight fluid ounces of water, milk, or other thin liquid will all also weigh eight ounces. However, this is not true for all ingredients, due to varying densities. For instance, one cup of flour weighs 4.25 ounces, while one cup of sugar weighs 7 ounces.

Measuring by Weight

Measuring by weight is by far the most accurate method. It doesn't matter how packed-together your ingredient is, 100 grams will always weigh 100 grams. The other beauty of measuring by weight is that you can measure every ingredient using the same method, and you only need one tool to do it: a scale!

Grams are my preferred unit for weight measurement. If you grew up in the US, I empathize with you about feeling unfamiliar with the metric system. However, grams are the smallest form of weight measurement, and therefore the most accurate. Don't fret! As long as you can read the numbers on a scale, you can easily measure in grams.

How to Measure Ingredients by Weight

1. Turn on your scale and select your unit of measurement. For all recipes in this book, select grams.
2. Set your bowl on top of the scale and press the "tare" button. This button zeroes out the scale, discounting the weight of your bowl. Make sure you zero out your scale before you measure out each ingredient.
3. Now you can proceed with putting your ingredient into the bowl to measure it out.

Measuring by Volume

Measuring by volume is a bit trickier than measuring by weight. Depending on how densely or loosely packed your ingredient is, more or less of it can take up the same amount of space. To avoid having too many issues with this, there are a few rules of thumb when measuring by volume.

Measuring Powdery Dry Ingredients

Things like flour, powdered sugar, cornstarch, cocoa powder, or any other powdery dry ingredient can cause the most issues when measuring by volume. To prevent this, there is a proper way to measure these ingredients.

1. Start by stirring and fluffing up the ingredient with a spoon. This helps to aerate it a bit and break up any clumps.
2. Lightly spoon the ingredient into your measuring cup, overfilling it, and being careful not to pack it down at all.
3. Use the handle of the spoon or a knife and level it off. This gives you a nicely measured dry ingredient.

 Note: To measure small amounts of powdery dry ingredients like spices, or baking soda and baking powder, spoon it out with the measuring spoon and level it off.

Measuring Brown Sugar

Brown sugar is the one ingredient in baking that requires a little bit of packing down when measuring. Brown sugar is moist and sticky and can clump up a bit when stored. Lightly pressing it into the measuring cup will help press out any air pockets to help with more consistent measuring.

How to Measure Brown Sugar by Volume

1. Scoop the brown sugar out with your measuring cup, overfilling the cup slightly.
2. Lightly pack down the brown sugar until it feels like it is filling the measuring cup. If you have excess, use a knife to level it off.

Measuring Liquid Ingredients

Liquid ingredients are one category where it is more commonly accepted to measure by volume, even by professional bakers. Liquids cannot be compressed the way solids can, therefore it is a bit easier to be accurate when measuring liquids by volume. That said, weight is always more accurate, and the recipes in this book will include both weight and volume measurements for all ingredients, including liquids.

How to Measure Liquid Ingredients by Volume

1. Make sure you are using a liquid measuring cup (one with a pour spout and markings on the side) rather than a dry measuring cup.
2. Get down to eye level with the cup and pour the liquid in until it reaches the mark of measurement. Looking at the mark from above will not give you an accurate measurement.

Measuring Solid Mix-Ins

Solid mix-ins, like chocolate chips, dried fruit, and nuts, are the other category where it is more commonly accepted to measure by volume. These things do not typically affect the fundamental structure of the baked good; rather, they are just there to add flavor and texture.

In this book, you will find some master recipes that lay out a variety of options for you to flavor your batter or dough. Some of these ingredients are given as volume measurements, as they all have different densities. You will have the freedom to decide how much you want to add to your baked goods with a few guidelines.

Mise en Place

It's time to discuss the most important lesson I learned in culinary school, which was the lesson of "Mise en Place." *Mise en place* translates to mean "putting in place" or "everything in its place." In the culinary world, it is a general guiding principle for how you prepare yourself in the kitchen.

It means starting with a clean workspace, getting all of your ingredients measured out, having all of your tools ready, and fully reading through the recipe. I can't even begin to guess how many times this lesson was drilled into our heads in school.

I can own up to the fact that many of the missteps I have made in the kitchen could have been avoided if I had practiced mise en place. A few things that have happened include forgetting to put an ingredient in my recipe, adding an ingredient twice, dumping in a full cup of salt thinking it was sugar, realizing I didn't have an ingredient when my batter was already half-mixed, and not planning enough time to finish my recipe. These are only a few of my examples, and things I want you to avoid.

Now that I am a professional baking educator, I practice and preach mise en place with conviction. This is without a doubt one of the biggest components of my success in the kitchen. If you take only one thing away from this book, please take mise en place!

Principles of Mise en Place

Mise en place is most commonly associated with measuring out all of your ingredients before you start baking. However, I have five principles that I teach as the best way to prepare before you start your recipe.

1: Read the Recipe Through Completely

By reading the recipe thoroughly, you can gain a clear understanding of the workflow of the recipe and the timing involved. I have learned this the hard way, by starting a recipe that needed several hours of chilling time that I did not plan for. Many baking recipes also call for room-temperature ingredients. Reading the recipe thoroughly before you start will prompt you to plan ahead for these things.

2: Gain a Clear Understanding of the Terminology and Techniques Used

After you have read the recipe through, identify any terminology or techniques used that you may not be familiar with. Maybe the recipe instructs you to "fold egg whites into your batter." Do you have a clear understanding of what "folding in" means? If the answer is "no," then familiarize yourself with this technique.

3: Start with a Clean Workspace

Start with a tidy workspace. At times, I have the urge to think, "I'm going to have to clean up after I make this recipe anyway, so I'll just wait to do it all together." But, remember that cup of salt I mentioned earlier? That happened because I didn't tidy up my workspace first. Lesson learned.

4: Gather Everything You Will Need and Measure Your Ingredients

Gather any equipment, utensils, and ingredients you will need. Then measure out all of your ingredients *before* you start combining them.

I have often heard the argument that this creates more dishes to wash. I get it. I wash *so many* dishes! But I'm here to tell you, this is going to prevent numerous problems.

By measuring out all of your ingredients before you start, you will make sure that you actually do have enough of all the ingredients you need on hand. It will also ensure that you don't accidentally forget to put an ingredient into your recipe, or accidentally add it in twice.

5: Do Any Other Prep Required

The last step before you start combining your ingredients is to do any other little preparation steps that are going to set you up for success. Preheat your oven. Prepare your pans with parchment paper or non-stick spray, if applicable. Do things like zesting and juicing your citrus and cutting up your butter if your recipe calls for them.

You are now ready to start your recipe. I know it may seem like a lot of steps but getting into this habit is going to dramatically affect your consistency with your bakes. It also makes the entire baking experience more relaxed.

Baker Bettie's
Essential Rules of Better Baking

Now that you are ready to start baking, I have a few essential rules to keep in mind as you bake your way through the book!

Rule 1: Recipes Are Guidelines

While baking is a science, it should also be noted that recipes are guidelines and not set in stone. Everyone has different ingredients and tools available to them, along with a different environment. These things can affect how long something needs to bake or rise. Pay attention to your baked goods throughout the process so you can use your best judgment if adjustments need to be made.

Rule 2: Always Ask Why

The most important part of baking better is understanding why things are done. If you're using a technique or an ingredient and you don't understand its function, ask why. In this book we will cover most of the "whys" you will need to know. This is the most fundamental part of gaining baking confidence.

Rule 3: Technique Is Everything

A recipe is only as good as the technique used to execute it. In this book, we will focus heavily on technique. I encourage you to not skip over these sections, as it will greatly improve how consistent your results are with your bakes.

Rule 4: Keep Your Oven Door Shut!

One of the most common mistakes I see people make is opening their oven door too often during the baking process. Every time you open the oven door, a great deal of heat and steam is released. This can cause your baked goods to collapse, not rise as well, or take much longer to finish baking. Use the light in your oven to check on your baked goods until right near the end of the baking time. You can then open the door to get a better look.

Rule 5: Assess Your Flops

Baking "flops" are one of the greatest opportunities for learning. Assess the situation and try your best to figure out what might have happened. Was it a technique issue? A measuring issue? A timing issue? A substitution that didn't work? Figuring out what might have gone wrong is the best way to prevent mistakes in the future.

Rule 6: Allow Yourself to Play

I often hear that people don't enjoy baking because they don't like to follow recipes so closely. I want you to know that I highly encourage creativity and experimentation with baking recipes. This book is set up in such a way as to show you how to use base recipes to play with variations. It is very rewarding to come up with your own variation and be able to execute that well.

Rule 7: Practice, Practice, Practice!

As with any new skill, becoming a better baker takes practice. It is very rare that someone picks up a new skill and is automatically good at it. Push through the frustrating parts of the process and keep practicing! I'm going to walk you through it all, so you have a clear path!

Part 2

Mixing Methods & Master Recipes

In this section, we will be reviewing five major categories of baking. Each chapter will cover the major mixing methods used for each type of baked good, as well as important baking science to help you perfect the topic. Each chapter also includes master recipes that I have developed. When I'm creating recipes, my masters are where I start, and I tweak from there.

When I teach baking classes, I love letting my students in on this secret of the baking world. This approach to baking really builds confidence and opens up a much broader understanding of how baking works.

Chocolate Chip Banana Bread (page 98)

5

Quick Breads

I always encourage new bakers to start with quick breads because, not only are they simple to master, they really bring a sense of warmth and nostalgia to the home. There is nothing better on a Sunday morning than pulling a batch of perfectly fluffy blueberry muffins out of the oven.

Quick breads are different from yeast breads in texture and flavor, because they use chemical leavening (baking soda and/or baking powder) instead of yeast to make them rise. They tend to be cakier in texture, and often include more sugar than yeasted bread. Baked goods that fall in the quick bread category include muffins, pancakes, biscuits, scones, soda breads, and batter breads.

Unlike yeast breads, which need a long time to rise before baking, quick breads are baked soon after mixing. This is because baking soda and baking powder start producing leavening gases as soon as they are hydrated—hence the term "quick bread!"

Quick Bread Mixing Methods

There are two main mixing methods utilized for making quick breads: the Muffin Mixing Method and the Biscuit Mixing Method. Quick breads that are made from a batter generally use the Muffin Mixing Method, while quick breads that are made from a dough typically use the Biscuit Mixing Method.

The main difference you will notice between these two mixing methods is the use of liquid fat in the Muffin Method, versus the use of solid fat in the Biscuit Method. Fat always serves the purpose of adding richness and tenderness to baked goods. But it does function somewhat differently in liquid versus solid form.

With batter breads, we want the fat to be very cohesively mixed throughout. This creates a baked good that is fluffy with a very even crumb. In contrast, we want the fat to remain solid and in tiny pieces throughout quick breads made using the Biscuit Method. This creates a baked good with a flaky texture and a more uneven crumb.

Managing Gluten in Quick Breads

One thing that both quick bread mixing methods have in common is the goal of reducing gluten formation. Gluten is necessary to give our baked goods structure, but too much gluten will make the quick breads tough and chewy.

As soon as flour is hydrated, gluten begins forming. The more the batter or dough is worked, the more elastic this gluten network will become. This is desirable in yeast bread, which will be discussed in depth in Chapter 9. However, in a quick bread, we want the final product to stay fluffy and tender.

The biggest tip for making any kind of quick bread is to mix and handle the dough or batter as little as possible.

The Muffin Mixing Method

The Muffin Mixing Method is typically used for any quick breads that are made from a batter. This includes:

- Muffins
- Cornbread
- Batter breads (i.e., banana bread, zucchini bread)
- Waffles and pancakes

The goal of this mixing method is to create a cohesive batter without developing a lot of gluten. This is accomplished by mixing the dry ingredients together and the wet ingredients together before combining the two parts. This ensures very little mixing is needed once the final batter comes together.

Which Liquid Fat to Use?

Typically, a neutral-flavored oil (like canola, vegetable, safflower, or grapeseed) is used in recipes that utilize the Muffin Mixing Method. However, melted butter can also be used for added flavor.

Steps of the Muffin Mixing Method

Before starting, make sure all ingredients are at room temperature.

1. Whisk all of the dry ingredients together.
2. Whisk all of the wet ingredients together in a separate bowl.
3. Pour the wet ingredients into the dry ingredients.
4. Use a silicone spatula or mixing spoon (not a whisk) to mix only until the flour is absorbed. The batter does not need to be perfectly smooth; lumps are okay to avoid overmixing!
5. If using mix-ins, fold into the batter, stirring as little as possible.
6. Transfer to your prepared baking pan and bake immediately.

Baker Bettie's Better Baking Book

Tips for Lining Your Pans

For all muffins and batter breads, you can either spray your pans well with non-stick spray (or use butter or oil to grease them), or you can use paper liners or parchment paper. I personally prefer the latter.

To Line a Baking Pan with Parchment Paper:

1. Start with a square of parchment paper that is at least one inch wider than your pan all the way around it. Set your pan in the center of the paper.
2. Cut the four corners out of the parchment paper, using your pan as a guide.
3. Lightly grease your pan and then place your piece of parchment in it, pressing down into the oil to hold it in place.

SWEET BATTER BREAD MASTER RECIPE

Yield: 10–16 muffins (depending on mix-ins), or one loaf

Specialty Equipment: Muffin tins, or 8.5 x 4.5-inch (22 x 11-cm) loaf pan

Mixing Method: Muffin Mixing Method

Prep Time: 25 minutes

Cook Time: 18 minutes for muffins/1 hour for a loaf

Total Time: 43 minutes for muffins/1 hour 25 minutes for a loaf

- 240 grams (2 cups) all-purpose flour
- 200 grams (1 cup) granulated sugar
- 10 grams (1 tablespoon) baking powder
- ¼ teaspoon kosher salt
- 1 large egg, room temperature
- 151 grams (⅔ cup, 160 milliliters) milk (skim, 1 percent, 2 percent, whole, or dairy-free), room temperature
- 113 grams (½ cup, 120 milliliters) neutral-flavored oil (canola, vegetable, safflower, grapeseed)

My sweet batter bread master recipe is my go-to starting point for almost all of my muffin recipes. They turn out light and fluffy, with those beautiful domes on top. You can also use this to make a full loaf of sweet quick bread.

Method

Prep:

1. At least 30 minutes before baking, measure out the milk and set it out with the egg to come to room temperature. Measure out the rest of the ingredients.

2. Position an oven rack to the center position. Preheat the oven to 400°F/205°C if making muffins or 350°F/175°C if making a loaf.

3. Prep your muffin tin(s) with muffin liners (the base recipe will make about 10 muffins, and if you add 2 cups of optional mix-ins, it will make 14–16 muffins). Alternatively, prep an 8.5 x 4.5-inch (22 x 11-cm) loaf pan with parchment paper or non-stick spray.

To Make the Batter:

1. In a large mixing bowl, whisk together the flour, sugar, baking powder, salt, and any spices if using.

2. In a separate bowl, lightly whisk together the egg, milk, oil, and any extracts, juices, and/or zests if using until well combined.

3. Pour the wet ingredients into the dry ingredient bowl.

4. Stir with a spoon or rubber spatula until just combined. This should only take about 30 seconds of mixing. The batter will be lumpy.

5. If using any solid mix-ins, gently fold them into the batter.

6. Divide the batter evenly between the muffin cups, filling to about ½ inch from the top, or pour into your loaf tin. If using, sprinkle the sugar or streusel topping liberally on each muffin or on top of your loaf.

7. **For muffins,** bake at 400°F/205°C for 15–18 minutes. **For a loaf,** bake at 350°F/175°C for 50–60 minutes, until lightly golden brown and the tops spring back when gently pushed, or a toothpick inserted in the center comes out clean. Check on your bake at about the halfway mark, and if it looks as though it is not baking evenly, rotate the pan.

8. **For muffins,** set the muffin trays on a rack to cool for at least 10 minutes before serving. **For a loaf,** transfer the baked loaf out of the pan onto a cooling rack about 10 minutes after taking it out of the oven. Let it cool for at least 20 minutes before slicing. This will help the texture of the bread to solidify.

9. If using a glaze, drizzle it on right before serving.

10. Store uneaten muffins or bread covered in foil or plastic wrap at room temperature for up to 3 days.

Flavor Variation Ideas

♦ **Blueberry Coffee Cake Loaf/Muffins:** Add 1 teaspoon cinnamon, 2 tablespoons lemon juice, 2 tablespoons lemon zest, 1½ teaspoons vanilla, and 250 grams (2 cups) fresh or frozen blueberries to the batter. Top with streusel (page 261) before baking.

♦ **Lemon Poppy Seed Loaf/Muffins:** Add 2 tablespoons lemon juice, 2 tablespoons lemon zest, and 2 tablespoons poppy seeds to the batter. Top with a lemon glaze (page 258) after cooling for at least 10 minutes.

 Baking Science Note: Muffins are baked at a higher temperature than a full loaf because the higher heat rapidly evaporates the liquid in the batter. This allows the muffins to rise quickly and dome before the crust sets. For a full loaf, lower heat is required so the outside of the bread does not burn before the middle of the loaf is cooked through.

Flavoring Your Muffins/Bread

Use this chart of flavoring options as a guide for flavoring your batter if desired. Mix and match as you like.

Extracts & Zests

(Use 1–2 of these if desired)

- 1 ½ teaspoons vanilla extract
- ½ teaspoon almond extract
- ¼ teaspoon anise extract
- 2 tablespoons lemon, lime, or orange zest + 2 tablespoons lemon, lime, or orange juice

Spices

(Use up to 2 ½ teaspoons total of combined spices if desired)

- 1–2 teaspoons cinnamon
- ½ teaspoon ginger
- ¼ teaspoon nutmeg
- ¼ teaspoon cardamom
- ⅛ teaspoon clove
- ⅛ teaspoon allspice

Solid Mix-Ins

(Use up to 2 cups total of solid mix-ins if desired.
Choose as many as you like within this total volume.)

- chocolate chips or chunks (milk, semi-sweet, dark, white)
- dried fruit (cranberries, cherries, raisins)
- fresh or frozen berries (raspberries, blueberries, cherries, diced strawberries, blackberries)
- chopped nuts (walnuts, pecans, almonds, pistachios)
- shredded coconut
- poppy seeds (only use up to 2 tablespoons)

Topping Options

(Use one of these toppings if desired)

- sugar topping (granulated or coarse sugar like turbinado; sprinkle liberally on tops before baking)
- streusel topping (page 261, add to tops right before baking)
- powdered sugar glaze (page 257, drizzle over tops after cooled)

Parmesan Herb Quick Bread (page 94)

SAVORY BATTER BREAD MASTER RECIPE

Yield: One loaf

Specialty Equipment: 8.5 x 4.5-inch (22 x 11-cm) loaf pan

Mixing Method: Muffin Mixing Method

Prep Time: 25 minutes

Cook Time: 50 minutes

Total Time: 1 hour 15 minutes

- 240 grams (2 cups) all-purpose flour
- 13 grams (1 tablespoon) granulated sugar
- 10 grams (1 tablespoon) baking powder
- 4 grams (¾ teaspoon) kosher salt
- 1 large egg, room temperature
- 227 grams (1 cup, 240 milliliters) milk (skim, 1 percent, 2 percent, whole, or dairy-free), room temperature
- 113 grams (½ cup, 120 milliliters) neutral-flavored oil, like canola, vegetable, safflower, or grapeseed—or olive oil can be used for additional flavor

This savory batter bread is very different from traditional yeasted bread. The texture is much more muffin-like—fluffier and less chewy than a yeasted bread. Batter breads are such a great way to play around with flavors without spending hours waiting for your bread dough to rise.

Method

Prep:

1. At least 30 minutes before baking, measure out the milk and set it out with the egg to come to room temperature. Measure out the rest of the ingredients.

2. Position an oven rack to the center position. Preheat the oven to 350°F/175°C.

3. Prep an 8.5 x 4.5-inch (22 x 11-cm) loaf pan with parchment paper or non-stick spray.

To Make the Bread:

1. In a large mixing bowl, whisk together the flour, sugar, baking powder, salt, and any spices or herbs if using.

2. In a separate bowl, lightly whisk together the egg, milk, and oil until well combined.

3. Pour the wet ingredients into the dry ingredients.

4. Use a spoon or rubber spatula (not a whisk) and stir until just combined. This should only take about 30–45 seconds of mixing. The batter will be lumpy. Do not overmix, or the bread will become tough.

5. If using any solid mix-ins, gently fold them into the batter.

6. Pour the batter into the prepared loaf pan. If desired, sprinkle a few of the solid mix-ins that you used on top for visual appeal.

7. Bake at 350°F/175°C for 42–50 minutes, until lightly golden brown and the top springs back when gently pushed, or a toothpick inserted in the center comes out clean. Check on your bake at about the halfway mark, and if it looks as though it is not baking evenly, rotate the pan.

8. Gently transfer the baked loaf out of the pan onto a cooling rack about 10 minutes after taking it out of the oven. Let it cool for at least 20 minutes before slicing. This will help the texture to solidify.

9. Store uneaten bread at room temperature, loosely wrapped in foil or plastic wrap, for up to 3 days.

Flavor Variation Ideas

- ♦ **Parmesan Herb Bread:** Add 1 teaspoon dried oregano, 1 teaspoon dried rosemary, 1 teaspoon dried thyme, ½ teaspoon garlic powder, and 200 grams (2 cups) shredded parmesan to the batter. Sprinkle the top with more parmesan before baking.

- ♦ **Cheddar Dill Bread:** Use buttermilk in place of the regular milk. Add 1 ½ teaspoons garlic powder, 1 teaspoon onion powder, 1 tablespoons dried dill, and 200 grams (2 cups) shredded sharp cheddar cheese to the batter. Sprinkle the top with more cheddar before baking.

Flavoring Your Bread

Use this chart of flavoring options as a guide for flavoring your bread if desired. Mix and match as you like.

Spices

(Use up to 2 ½ teaspoons total of combined spices if desired)

- 1 teaspoon cayenne pepper
- 1 teaspoon garlic powder
- 1 teaspoon onion powder
- ½ teaspoon paprika
- 1 teaspoon chili powder
- 1 teaspoon cumin

Herbs *(fresh or dried)*

(Use up to 1 tablespoon total of dried herbs or 3 tablespoons total of fresh herbs if desired)

- rosemary
- thyme
- sage
- oregano
- basil
- dill
- chives

Solid Mix-Ins

(Use up to 2 cups total of solid mix-ins if desired. You can choose as many as you like within this total volume.)

- chopped nuts (walnuts, almond, pistachios, pecans)
- shredded cheese (cheddar, Gruyere, Parmesan, mozzarella)
- sun-dried tomato, finely chopped (up to ¼ cup)
- pumpkin seeds or sunflower seeds *(Note: seeds like flax, chia, or sesame are not recommended as they absorb too much liquid)*
- oats (only use up to ½ cup, old-fashioned, or quick oats)
- dried fruit (cranberries, cherries, apricots, currants, raisins)
- fresh or pickled jalapeno, finely diced (up to ¼ cup)
- chopped olives, any kind you like (drain well, use up to 1 cup)

Cheddar Dill Quick Bread (page 94)

Zucchini Muffins (page 98)

FRUIT or VEG QUICK BREAD MASTER RECIPE

Yield: 12–16 muffins (depending on mix-ins you use), or 1 loaf

Specialty Equipment: Muffin tins or 8.5 x 4.5-inch (22 x 11-cm) loaf pan

Mixing Method: Muffin Mixing Method

Prep Time: 25 minutes

Cook Time: 20 minutes for muffins/1 hour 10 minutes for a loaf

Total Time: 45 minutes for muffins/1 hour 35 minutes for a loaf

- 240 grams (2 cups) all-purpose flour
- 200 grams (1 cup) granulated sugar
- 10 grams (1 tablespoon) baking powder
- 2 grams (½ teaspoon) kosher salt
- 113 grams (½ cup, 120 milliliters) neutral oil (vegetable, canola, safflower, grapeseed)
- 2 large eggs, room temperature
- 2 teaspoons vanilla extract
- 85 grams (6 tablespoons, 90 milliliters) milk (skim, 1 percent, 2 percent, whole, or dairy-free), room temperature
- 2 cups vegetable or fruit base (see chart for weight measurements)

Fruit and vegetable quick breads (like banana bread or zucchini bread) are incredibly versatile and forgiving. While most ingredients must be measured very accurately in baking, the fruit or vegetable base you choose does not need to be. If you have a little more or less than the recipe calls for, it will work out just fine. This is one of my favorite master recipes to work from because it is so versatile!

Method

Prep:

1. At least 30 minutes before baking, measure out the milk and set it out with the egg to come to room temperature. Measure out the rest of the ingredients.

2. Position an oven rack to the center position. Preheat the oven to 400°F/205°C if making muffins and 350°F/175°C if making a loaf.

3. Prep your muffin tin(s) with muffin liners (the base recipe will make about 12 muffins, and if you add 2½ cups of optional mix-ins, it will make 14–16 muffins). Alternatively, prep an 8.5 x 4.5-inch (22 x 11-cm) loaf pan with parchment paper or non-stick spray.

To Make the Batter:

1. In a large mixing bowl, whisk together the flour, sugar, baking powder, salt, and any spices if using.

2. In a separate bowl, lightly whisk together the oil, egg, vanilla extract, milk, vegetable or fruit base, and any extracts, juices, and/or zests if using until well combined.

3. Pour the wet ingredients into the dry ingredient bowl.

4. Stir with a spoon or silicone spatula until just combined. This should only take about 30–45 seconds of mixing. The batter will be pretty thick and lumpy. Do not overmix, or the bread will become tough.

5. If using any solid mix-ins, gently fold them into the batter.

6. Divide the batter evenly between the muffin cups, leaving about ½ inch from the top, or pour into your loaf tin. If using, sprinkle the sugar or streusel topping liberally on each muffin or on top of your loaf.

7. **For muffins,** bake at 400°F/205°C for 16–20 minutes. **For a loaf,** bake at 350°F/175°C for 60–70 minutes, until lightly golden brown and the tops spring back when gently pushed, or a toothpick inserted in the center comes out clean. Check on your bake at about the halfway mark, and if it looks as though it is not baking evenly, rotate the pan.

8. **For muffins,** set the muffin trays on a rack to cool for at least 10 minutes before serving. **For a loaf,** transfer the baked loaf out of the pan onto a cooling rack about 10 minutes after taking it out of the oven. Let it cool for at least 20 minutes before slicing. This will help the texture of the bread to solidify.

9. If using a glaze, drizzle it on right before serving.

10. Store uneaten muffins or bread, covered in foil or plastic wrap, at room temperature for up to 3 days.

Flavor Variation Ideas

- **Chocolate Chip Banana Bread/Muffins:** Use mashed banana as the base ingredient. Use dark brown sugar in place of the granulated sugar. Add 1½ teaspoons cinnamon, ¼ teaspoon nutmeg, and 175 grams (1 cup) mini chocolate chips to the batter. Sprinkle with turbinado sugar before baking.

- **Zucchini Bread/Muffins:** Use shredded zucchini as the base ingredient; add 1½ teaspoons cinnamon, ¼ teaspoon nutmeg, 2 tablespoons lemon juice, 1 tablespoon lemon zest, and 100 grams (1 cup) toasted chopped walnuts (page 256) to the batter.

- **Loaded Carrot Bread/Muffins:** Use shredded carrot as the base ingredient; add 1½ teaspoons cinnamon, 1½ tablespoon orange zest, 2 tablespoons orange juice, 100 grams (1 cups) toasted chopped pecans (page 256), 150 grams (1 cup) raisins, and 50 grams (½ cup) shredded sweetened coconut to the batter.

- **Apple Spice Oat Bread/Muffins:** Use shredded apple as the base ingredient; add 1½ teaspoons cinnamon, ½ teaspoon nutmeg, ½ teaspoon ginger, and 100 grams (1 cup) oats to the batter. Top with oat streusel (page 261) before baking.

Flavoring Your Batter

Use this chart of flavoring options as a guide for flavoring your bread. Mix and match as you like.

Fruit or Veg Base

(**Required**, *choose one base for your batter*)

- 480 grams (2 cups) mashed ripe banana
- 480 grams (2 cups) pumpkin puree
- 225 grams (2 cups) shredded carrot
- 225 grams (2 cups) shredded apple (peeled or unpeeled)
- 225 grams (2 cups) shredded zucchini (courgette) or yellow summer squash (peeled or unpeeled)

Spices

(*Use up to 2½ teaspoons of combined spices if desired*)

- 1½ teaspoons cinnamon
- ½ teaspoon nutmeg
- ½ teaspoon ginger
- ¼ teaspoon clove
- ¼ teaspoon allspice
- 2 teaspoons pumpkin pie spice
- 2 teaspoons apple pie spice

Extracts & Zests

(*Use 1–2 of these if desired*)

- ½ teaspoon almond extract
- ¼ teaspoon anise extract
- 2 tablespoons lemon, lime, or orange juice + 2 tablespoons lemon, lime, or orange zest

Solid Mix-Ins

(*Use up to 2½ cups total solid mix-ins if desired. Choose as many as you like within this volume. Recommended: only use up to 2 cups of any single mix-in*)

- chocolate chips or chunks (milk, semi-sweet, dark, white)
- chopped nuts (walnuts, pecans, almonds, pistachios)
- oats (only use up to 1 cup, old-fashioned or quick oats)
- dried fruit (cranberries, cherries, raisins, currants)
- shredded coconut

Topping Options

(*Use one of these toppings if desired*)

- sugar topping (granulated or coarse sugar like turbinado sugar, sprinkle liberally on tops before baking)
- streusel topping (page 261, add to tops right before baking)
- powdered sugar glaze (page 257, drizzle over tops after cooling)

CORNBREAD MASTER RECIPE

Yield: 9 servings

Specialty Equipment:

8-inch (20-cm) square or round baking pan or muffin tins

Mixing Method: Muffin Mixing Method

Prep Time: 20 minutes

Cook Time: 18 minutes for muffins/28 minutes for square pan

Total Time: 38 minutes for muffins/48 minutes for square pan

- 180 grams (1 ½ cups) cornmeal
- 90 grams (¾ cup) all-purpose flour
- 5 grams (1 ½ teaspoons) baking powder
- ½ teaspoon baking soda
- 7 grams (1 ½ teaspoons) kosher salt
- 113 grams (½ cup, 1 stick) unsalted butter
- 85 grams (¼ cup, 60 milliliters) honey
- 360 grams (1 ½ cups, 360 milliliters) buttermilk, room temperature
- 2 large eggs, at room temperature

Cornbread is one of those classic baked goods in the US that is rooted in a lot of history and tradition. Many families have their own recipe that has been passed down from generation to generation, and there are varying thoughts on how it should be made. Some prefer a straight cornmeal cornbread without any flour, while others prefer a fluffier and sweeter version. This recipe is a bit in the middle. It is heavy on the cornmeal ratio, because I really want that flavor to be the star, but it does incorporate some flour and just a touch of honey to round out the flavors. Most often, I make the plain version of this recipe. However, it also works beautifully as a master recipe to create endless flavors.

Method

Prep:

1. At least 30 minutes before baking, measure out the buttermilk and set it out with the eggs to come to room temperature. Measure out the rest of your ingredients. Melt the butter and set aside to cool slightly.
2. Position the oven rack to the center position. Preheat the oven to 400°F/205°C.
3. Prepare an 8-inch (20-cm) square or round baking pan or muffin tins with non-stick spray. Muffin liners do not work well with this recipe, as the papers stick too much to the cornbread.

To Make the Cornbread:

1. In a large mixing bowl, combine the cornmeal, flour, baking soda, baking powder, salt, and any herbs or spices if using.
2. In a separate bowl, whisk together the melted butter, honey, eggs, and buttermilk.
3. Add the wet ingredients into the dry ingredient bowl.
4. Stir with a mixing spoon or silicone spatula until everything is just incorporated. Avoid overmixing.
5. If using any solid mix-ins, fold them in here.

6. Pour the batter into your prepared pan or divide evenly between the muffin tins (this should make about 9–10 muffins).

7. Cook at 400°F/205°C for about 23–28 minutes for an 8-inch (20-cm) square or round pan and 16–18 minutes for muffins—until a tester comes out clean from the center. If you would like a crispy top crust, turn the broiler on for 1–2 minutes. Watch very closely.

8. As an optional step, rub a stick of butter over the top of the cornbread just when it comes out of the oven. This helps keep it extra moist and flavorful.

9. Store uneaten cornbread at room temperature, loosely wrapped in foil or plastic wrap. Best eaten within 2 days.

Flavor Variation Ideas

♦ **Jalapeno Cheddar Cornbread:** Add 1 teaspoon garlic powder to the dry ingredients. Fold in 125 grams (1¼ cups lightly packed) shredded sharp cheddar cheese, and 80 grams (⅔ cup, about 4 small or 2 large) deseeded and minced jalapenos.

♦ **Smoky Chipotle Cornbread:** Add 1 teaspoon onion powder to the dry ingredients. Add 1½ tablespoons adobo sauce (from canned chipotle in adobo) to the wet ingredients. Fold in 125 grams (1 cup) fresh or frozen corn kernels, and 2 chipotle peppers in adobo, deseeded and minced.

Flavoring Your Cornbread

Use this chart of flavoring options as a guide for flavoring your bread if desired. Mix and match as you like.

Spices *(Use up to 2½ teaspoons total of combined spices if desired)*

- 1 teaspoon cayenne pepper
- 1 teaspoon garlic powder
- 1 teaspoon onion powder
- 1 teaspoon paprika
- 1 teaspoon chili powder
- 1 teaspoon cumin

Herbs *(fresh or dried) (Use up to 1 tablespoon total of dried herbs or 3 tablespoons total of fresh herbs if desired)*

- rosemary
- thyme
- sage
- oregano
- basil
- dill
- chives

Solid Mix-Ins *(Use up to 2 cups total of solid mix-ins if desired. You can choose as many as you like within this volume.)*

- shredded cheese (cheddar, gruyere, parmesan, mozzarella)
- sun-dried tomato, finely chopped (up to ¼ cup)
- roasted red peppers, finely chopped (up to ¼ cup)
- fresh or pickled jalapeno, finely diced (only up to ½ cup)
- roasted green chiles, chopped and drained (Hatch or Anaheim)
- 2–3 chipotle peppers in adobo, seeded and minced
- crumbled cooked bacon
- fresh or frozen corn kernels

The Biscuit Mixing Method

The Biscuit Mixing Method is used for quick breads that are made from a dough. This includes:

- Biscuits
- Scones
- Soda breads

Solid fat is utilized in this method, and it is "cut into" the flour mixture. This serves two purposes:

The first purpose is to *coat the flour with fat*, which acts as a barrier to the liquid that will be added later, slowing gluten formation. This will keep your quick bread tender.

The second purpose is to *distribute small solid pieces of fat throughout the dough*. These pieces of fat will melt in the oven, creating little pockets of flakiness throughout the final baked good.

Which Solid Fat to Use?

There are a variety of solid fat options to use in your quick breads. Butter, shortening, and lard are the most commonly used.

Butter creates a quick bread with the most rise because of its water content. When butter melts in the oven, water evaporates from it, creating steam and thus more rise in your baked goods. Butter also has a melting point around body temperature, which can make for a more pleasant eating experience since it melts in your mouth.

Shortening and lard are both 100 percent fat and do not have any water present in them. This means that, while they do not allow quick breads to rise quite as high, the extra fat present *creates an even more tender and flaky texture*. However, these fats can leave a bit of a film in the mouth if not eaten while warm, due to their higher melting point.

With this knowledge, you can decide which fats have the characteristics you are looking for in your quick bread. You may even decide to use a combination of two!

Steps of the Biscuit Mixing Method

Before starting, make sure the butter, liquid, and eggs (if in the recipe) are very cold.

Baker Bettie's Better Baking Book

1. Whisk together the dry ingredients.

2. Use a pastry blender, fork, or your fingertips to cut the fat throughout the flour mixture. To do this, press down on the fat with the wires of the pastry blender as you move it around the bowl.

3. Continue cutting the fat into the flour until most of the pieces of fat are about the size of peas, with some pieces being about the size of a walnut half.

4. If you are adding solid mix-ins (like fruit or nuts), toss them into the flour mixture after the fat is cut in.

5. Combine all of the wet ingredients together and add to the mixing bowl.

6. Mix the wet ingredients into the dry ingredients very gently. The dough will look very incohesive and "shaggy."

7. Transfer the dough to a lightly floured work surface and press it together into one mass.

8. Depending on the recipe, either lightly knead or gently fold the dough (more detailed step-by-step images of this process are in the following recipes).

9. Shape the dough into desired forms. Be gentle as you shape so that you do not overwork the gluten structure.

 Note: If the dough does not feel cold, place it in the freezer for a few minutes before baking to resolidify the fat.

Folding vs. Kneading in Biscuit Mixing Method

The Biscuit Mixing Method calls for the dough to be either lightly kneaded or folded over itself several times, depending on the recipe. Lightly kneading the dough will create a more cohesive texture. In contrast, folding the dough over itself creates layers in it, which will lead to a flakier final texture. This process mimics a more advanced pastry technique called "lamination" in which sheets of fat are folded into a dough over and over again to create many alternating layers of dough and fat.

BUTTERMILK BISCUIT RECIPE

Yield: 8 biscuits

Specialty Equipment:
Pastry blender, 2.5-inch
(6-cm) round cutter

Mixing Method: Biscuit
Mixing Method

Prep Time: 20 minutes

Cook Time: 15 minutes

Total Time: 35 minutes

- 240 grams (2 cups)
  all-purpose flour
- 10 grams (1 tablespoon)
  baking powder
- ¼ teaspoon baking soda
- 6 grams (1 ¼ teaspoons)
  kosher salt
- 25 grams (2 tablespoons)
  sugar, *optional*
- 85 grams (6 tablespoons) cold
  unsalted butter (cut into small
  pieces), or lard, or shortening
- 240 grams (1 cup, 240
  milliliters) buttermilk, cold

Buttermilk biscuits are one of the first things I learned to bake. I had only ever baked biscuits from the can before, and I was so impressed that I could make them from scratch. These biscuits can be made with butter, lard, or shortening. I typically use butter but often opt for lard if they will be served with sausage gravy. This recipe can also be made as a "drop biscuit," which is a bit easier and nice for a quick dinner side or is the perfect topping for a cobbler (see Chapter 8). I typically only add the optional sugar when making this dough as a cobbler topping, but some prefer a sweeter buttermilk biscuit.

Method

Prep:

1. Position an oven rack to the center position and preheat to 450°F/230°C.
2. Line a sheet pan with parchment paper or a silicone baking mat.
3. If you are using butter as the fat, cut it up into small pieces and put it back in the refrigerator to stay cold. Measure out the rest of the ingredients.

To Make the Biscuits:

1. In a large mixing bowl, whisk together the flour, baking powder, baking soda, salt, sugar (if using), and any herbs or spices if using.
2. Add the cold butter, lard, or shortening to the mixing bowl and cut it into the flour mixture. To do this, press down on the fat with the wires of the pastry blender or the tines of a fork as you move it around the bowl. Continue cutting the fat into the flour until most of the pieces of fat are about the size of peas, with some pieces being about the size of a walnut half.
3. If using, toss your solid mix-ins throughout the flour/butter mixture at this point.

4. Add the cold buttermilk into the bowl and stir with a spoon or a silicone spatula just until combined. This should only take a few turns. The dough will be pretty wet and sticky.

5. Turn the dough out onto a lightly floured counter. Dust flour over the top of the dough. With floured hands, bring the dough together into one mass.

6. Pat the dough out (do not roll with a rolling pin) until it is about 1 inch (2.5 cm) thick. Using a bench knife (or a metal spatula if you do not have a bench knife), fold the dough in half and then turn it 90 degrees. Pat out and fold again, repeating, for a total of 6 times. This process is creating layers that will make flaky biscuits.

7. Press the dough out to about 1 inch (2.5 cm) thick and use a round cutter that is about 2.5 inches (6 cm) in diameter to cut out your biscuits. When cutting out, dip your cutter in flour, press straight down, and pull it back up without twisting it. Twisting can seal the edge of your biscuit, not allowing it to rise fully. Gently pat the scraps together to cut out the rest of your biscuits. Alternatively, you can pat the dough into a rectangle and use a sharp knife to divide the dough into 8 rectangular-shaped biscuits.

8. Place the biscuits on a parchment-lined baking sheet with the edges touching so they will rise up against each other.

9. As an optional step, place the sheet pan in the freezer for 10 minutes before baking. This will ensure that your biscuits will not spread too much and will allow your oven to fully preheat.

10. Bake at 450°F/230°C for 13–15 minutes until golden brown. Do not open the oven door for *at least* the first half of baking time. You want the steam to stay trapped in the oven to help with the rise.

11. Brush biscuits with melted butter and sprinkle with flaky salt if desired.

12. Biscuits are best eaten fresh, but they can also be stored, once completely cooled, at room temperature and wrapped in foil for 2 days. Alternatively, you can freeze the biscuits raw and bake straight from frozen at 425°F/220°C for 18–21 minutes, until baked through.

To Make Drop Biscuits: Mix the dough up to step 4. Use a 2-oz. cookie scoop or large spoon to drop large mounds of dough on a parchment-lined baking sheet. Bake as you would for traditional biscuits. These biscuits are simpler to make, but are a bit less flaky in texture, since the folds are not added to the dough.

Flavor Variation Ideas

♦ **Garlic Cheddar Biscuits:** Add ½ teaspoon garlic powder and 200 grams (2 cups) shredded sharp cheddar cheese to the dough. Melt 28 grams (2 tablespoons) unsalted butter and combine with ½ teaspoon garlic powder, and ½ teaspoon kosher salt. Brush over the biscuits when they come out of the oven.

♦ **Fresh Herb Biscuits:** Add in 1 tablespoon each of fresh minced rosemary, thyme, and sage to the dry ingredients. These biscuits are phenomenal with sausage gravy.

 Baking Science Note: Baking biscuits at such a high heat helps the crust set quickly, so the biscuits rise up instead of spreading out. This also traps the butter inside the crust, so it doesn't ooze out of the biscuit while baking. The same method is used for scones.

Blueberry Lemon Scones (page 113) with Lemon Glaze (page 258)

SCONE MASTER RECIPE

Yield: 8 scones

Specialty Equipment:
Pastry blender

Mixing Method: Biscuit
Mixing Method

Prep Time: 20 minutes

Cook Time: 18 minutes

Total Time: 38 minutes

- 240 grams (2 cups)
  all-purpose flour
- 100 grams (½ cup)
  granulated sugar
- 10 grams (1 tablespoon)
  baking powder
- 2 grams (½ teaspoon)
  kosher salt
- 113 grams (½ cup, 1 stick)
  very cold unsalted butter,
  cut into small cubes
- 1 large egg, cold
- 117 grams (½ cup, 120
  ml) heavy cream, cold
- a few tablespoons of
  additional heavy cream
  for brushing the tops

These are American bakery-style scones that are slightly fluffier, sweeter, and closer to a pastry than many scones found outside the US. These are also often topped with a powdered sugar glaze. Additionally, scones can be made plain and eaten with whatever fillings you like or used as the base of strawberry shortcake.

Method

Prep:

1. Position an oven rack to the center position. Preheat the oven to 425°F/220°C. Make sure you give the oven ample time to preheat, as the scones will spread too much if it isn't hot enough.

2. Line a sheet pan with parchment paper or a silicone baking mat.

3. Cut up the butter into small pieces and put it back in the refrigerator to stay cold. Measure out the rest of your ingredients. If you are using frozen berries as a mix-in, keep them in the freezer until you add them to your dough. They need to be completely frozen or they will release too much moisture, making the dough unmanageable.

To Make the Scones:

1. In a large bowl whisk together the flour, sugar, baking powder, salt, and any spices if using.

2. Add the pieces of cold butter to the mixing bowl and cut it into the flour mixture. To do this, press down on the fat with the wires of the pastry blender or the tines of a fork as you move it around the bowl. Continue cutting the fat into the flour until most of the pieces of fat are about the size of peas, with some pieces being about the size of a walnut half.

3. If using, toss the solid mix-ins throughout the flour/butter mixture at this point.

4. Lightly whisk together the heavy cream, the egg, and any zests or extracts if using.

5. Pour the wet ingredients into the dry ingredients and mix with a silicone spatula just until the liquid is absorbed. This should only take a few turns.

The dough will look incohesive, but it will come together on the counter in the next step.

6. Turn the dough out onto a lightly floured countertop and flour the top of the dough. The dough is typically very crumbly at this point; this is normal. Use a bit of pressure to press the dough together into one mass.

7. Press the dough out to about a 1-inch-(2.5-cm)-thick rectangle.

8. Using a bench knife (or a metal spatula can be helpful if you do not have a bench knife), fold the dough in half and then turn it 90 degrees. Pat out and fold again for a total of 6 times. The dough will likely crumble during the first few turns. Be very gentle and keep patting it back together. This process is creating layers which will create flaky scones. If you use frozen berries, it can make this dough moister and trickier to work with. Dust more flour on top of the dough as needed to make it manageable.

9. Pat the dough out to about a 7-inch (18-cm) circle (about 1.5-inch, 4-cm thick). Cut into 8 triangle-shaped pieces. I like to use a bench knife for this, but a sharp knife also works. Transfer the scones onto a baking sheet lined with parchment paper or a silicone baking mat. Brush lightly with cream and sprinkle liberally with turbinado or granulated sugar, if desired.

10. As an optional step, place the sheet pan in the freezer for 10 minutes before baking. This will ensure that your scones will not spread too much and will allow your oven to fully preheat.

11. Bake at 425°F/220°C for 14–18 minutes until golden brown and firm when gently pressed on.

12. Transfer to a cooling rack. If using a glaze, allow the scones to cool for at least 10 minutes before adding.

13. Store leftovers, completely cooled, at room temperature, wrapped in foil or plastic wrap, for up to 2 days. Alternatively, you can freeze the scones raw and bake straight from frozen at 425°F/220°C for 18–22 minutes, until baked through.

Baker Bettie's Better Baking Book

Flavor Variation Ideas

♦ **Blueberry Lemon Scones:** Add 125 grams (1 cup) fresh or frozen blueberries, 1 tablespoon lemon zest, and 1 tablespoon lemon juice to the dough. Top with coarse sugar before baking. Drizzle with lemon glaze if desired (page 258) after cooling for at least 10 minutes.

♦ **Cherry Almond Scones:** Add 115 grams (¾ cup) dried cherries or chopped fresh cherries, 30 grams (¼ cup) sliced almonds, and ¼ teaspoon almond extract to the dough. Top with coarse sugar before baking. Drizzle with almond glaze (page 257) after cooling for at least 10 minutes.

♦ **Strawberry Shortcakes:** Make the strawberry sauce (page 250) and set aside to let cool. Make plain scones cut into 2.5-inch (6-cm) circles (you should get about 6). Split the scones in half. Layer with whipped cream (page 263) and the strawberry sauce.

Flavoring Your Scones

Use this chart of flavoring options as a guide for flavoring your scones. Mix and match as you like.

Spices

(Use up to 1 ½ teaspoons total of combined spices, if desired)

- 1 teaspoon cinnamon
- ¼ teaspoon ginger
- ¼ teaspoon nutmeg
- ⅛ teaspoon clove

Extracts, Juices, & Zests

(Use 1–2 of these if desired)

- 1 teaspoon vanilla extract
- ¼ teaspoon almond extract
- ¼ teaspoon anise extract
- 1 tablespoon lemon, lime, or orange juice + 1 tablespoon lemon, lime, or orange zest

Solid Mix-Ins

(Use up to 1 cup total of solid mix-ins if desired. Choose as many as you like within this volume.)

- chocolate chips or chunks (milk, semi-sweet, dark, or white chocolate)
- dried fruit (cranberries, cherries, raisins)
- fresh or frozen berries (raspberries, blueberries, cherries, strawberries, blackberries)
- chopped nuts (walnuts, pecans, almonds, pistachios)
- shredded coconut
- poppy seeds (only use up to 1 tablespoon)

Topping Options

(Optional, the glaze can be used in addition to the sugar topping if you like)

- sugar topping *(granulated or coarse sugar like sanding sugar or turbinado sugar, sprinkle liberally on tops before baking)*
- powdered sugar glaze *(page 257, drizzle over tops when cool)*

Currant and Caraway Soda Bread (page 116)

SODA BREAD MASTER RECIPE

Yield: 8 servings

Specialty Equipment:

Pastry blender

Mixing Method: Biscuit

Mixing Method

Prep Time: 20 minutes

Cook Time: 30 minutes

Total Time: 50 minutes

- 360 grams (3 cups)
  all-purpose flour
- 5 grams (1 teaspoon) kosher salt
- 5 grams (1 teaspoon)
  baking soda
- 50 grams (¼ cup) granulated
  sugar, *optional*
- 56 grams (4 tablespoons,
  ½ stick) unsalted butter, cold
  and cut into small pieces
- 320 grams (1⅓ cups, 320
  milliliters) buttermilk, cold

Soda bread is an easy bread that gets its name from the baking soda that does all of the leavening in the recipe. The texture of this bread is different from yeasted bread and much more like a scone. This is such a great quick bread to throw together to serve with a soup or stew.

Method

Prep:

1. Position the oven rack to the center position. Preheat the oven to 450°F/230°C.
2. Line a baking sheet with parchment paper and set aside. Measure out your ingredients.

To Make the Bread:

1. In a large mixing bowl whisk together the flour, salt, baking soda, sugar (if using), and any other herbs or spices if using.
2. Add the cold butter to the bowl and cut through the flour mixture. To do this, press down on the fat with the wires of the pastry blender or the tines of a fork as you move it around the bowl. Continue cutting the fat into the flour until it is all about the size of pebbles and the mixture looks like a coarse meal.
3. Add the buttermilk and stir with a rubber spatula until a soft dough forms.
4. Liberally flour a work surface and transfer the dough to it. Flour the top of the dough and your hands. Gather it together into one mass.
5. Knead the dough gently a few times by pushing it forward with the heels of your hands and then bringing it back toward you and folding it over itself, until you have a more cohesive dough. Only spend about 30 seconds on this to not overwork the gluten.
6. Transfer the dough to the prepared pan and shape it into a disk that is about 2.5 inches (6 cm) thick.
7. Use a sharp knife to cut a deep X across the dough, going almost all the way through to the pan.

8. Bake at 450°F/230°C for 26–30 minutes, until deep golden brown and a toothpick comes out clean from the center.

9. Brush melted butter over the top if desired.

10. Soda bread is best eaten warm from the oven. However, leftover bread can be wrapped in foil or plastic wrap, once cooled, and stored at room temperature for up to 2 days. Refresh in the oven for a few minutes to re-warm.

Flavor Variation Ideas

♦ **"Brown Bread" Soda Bread:** Reduce the all-purpose flour to 180 grams (1 ½ cups) and add 150 grams (1 ¼ cups) whole wheat flour. Toss 50 grams (½ cup) rolled oats in the flour/butter mixture before adding in the buttermilk. Brush the top with a bit of buttermilk and sprinkle with a few more oats before baking.

♦ **Currant and Caraway Soda Bread:** (This is a very traditional Irish combination.) Use the sugar in the recipe. Stir in 1 tablespoon caraway seeds and 150 grams (1 cup) of currants (or raisins) before adding in the buttermilk.

Brown Bread (page 116)

6

Cookies & Bars

Cookies are where my love for baking blossomed. A fresh chocolate chip cookie right out of the oven feels like a warm hug and therefore, they were the first baked good I perfected.

Cookies come in an infinite number of varieties, and because of this, there are not as many cut-and-dried base recipes as there are with quick breads. Many cookie recipes are singular in their use. However, the mixing methods are pretty straightforward, and you will be able to carry them over to use with your favorite recipes.

Cookie Mixing Methods

If you have ever made homemade brownies or chocolate chip cookies, then you have likely already utilized the main mixing methods that will cover the bulk of all cookies and bars: the One-Bowl Method for Cookies and the Creaming Method for Cookies. Notice that I specify "for cookies" for each of these methods. This is because there are versions of these mixing methods that are utilized specifically for cakes as well, but they vary slightly in their process.

The One-Bowl Method

The main difference between the One-Bowl Method and the Creaming Method is the use of liquid fat in the One-Bowl Method. This method does not require a hand mixer or stand mixer—it can be mixed using simply a bowl and a mixing spoon.

The One-Bowl Method is typically utilized for cookies and bars with a chewy texture, which includes brownies and blondies as well as some forms of drop cookies. This method is extremely forgiving due to the fact that butter and sugar are not being creamed together, which requires much more attention to the process.

Steps in the One-Bowl Method for Cookies

Before starting, have the eggs at room temperature. If applicable, melt the butter.

1. Mix the sugar and liquid fat together until well combined.
2. Add the eggs and any extracts.
3. Add the dry ingredients into the bowl and mix to combine.
4. Transfer to the prepared baking pan and bake.

Image by Lisa Kay Creative Photography

CLASSIC FUDGY BROWNIE RECIPE

Yield: 9 brownies

Specialty Equipment: 8-inch (20-cm) square baking pan

Mixing Method: The One-Bowl Method for Cookies

Prep Time: 20 minutes

Cook Time: 33 minutes

Total Time: 53 minutes

- 113 grams (½ cup, 1 stick) unsalted butter, melted and hot
- 100 grams (½ cup) granulated sugar
- 150 grams (¾ cup) brown sugar (preferably dark brown sugar)
- 53 grams (⅔ cup) natural cocoa powder
- 2 large eggs, room temperature
- 2 teaspoons vanilla extract
- 2 grams (½ teaspoon) kosher salt
- ⅛ teaspoon baking soda
- 85 grams (½ cup + 3 tablespoons) all-purpose flour
- 55 grams (2 ounces) semi-sweet or bittersweet chocolate, finely chopped

This is my favorite simple scratch brownie recipe. I personally love the texture of brownies that come from box mix and wanted this recipe to replicate that—super chewy in the middle, with crisp edges, and the perfect amount of fudginess.

Method

Prep:

1. At least 30 minutes before baking, take the eggs out of the refrigerator to come to room temperature. Measure out the rest of the ingredients. Finely chop the chocolate with a serrated knife.

2. Position an oven rack in the center position. Preheat the oven to 325°F/165°C.

3. Line an 8-inch (20-cm) square pan with parchment paper or grease with non-stick spray.

To Make the Brownies:

1. Melt the butter either in the microwave or in a saucepan on the stove. The butter needs to be very hot!

2. In a large mixing bowl, whisk together the granulated sugar, brown sugar, and cocoa powder. Add the hot melted butter and whisk to combine.

3. Add the vanilla extract and the eggs, whisking vigorously for about 30 seconds.

4. Add the salt, baking soda, and flour to the bowl and stir with a mixing spoon or silicone spatula for about 30 seconds to help develop the gluten/chewiness.

5. Fold in the chopped chocolate, saving about a quarter of it to sprinkle on top before baking.

6. Transfer the mixture into your prepared pan and spread evenly. Top with the reserved chocolate.

7. Bake at 325°F/165°C for 28–33 minutes until a toothpick inserted in the center comes out with moist crumbs clinging to it.

8. Set the pan on a cooling rack to cool for at least 15 minutes before slicing. The brownies will not be solidified when they first come out of the oven.

9. Store leftover brownies at room temperature in an airtight container for 4–5 days.

Flavor Variation Ideas

♦ **Salted Caramel Pecan Brownies:** Add 50 grams (½ cup) of toasted chopped pecans (page 256) to the batter. When the brownies come out of the oven, drizzle 140 grams (½ cup, 120 milliliters) warm caramel sauce (store-bought or homemade, page 251) over the batter and sprinkle kosher or coarse sea salt over the top. Allow the caramel sauce to set for at least 15 minutes before slicing.

♦ **Spiced Hot Chocolate Brownies:** Add ½ teaspoon cinnamon and ¼ teaspoon cayenne when you add the dry ingredients to the batter.

 Baking Science Note: The hot butter used in this recipe will "bloom" the cocoa powder, bringing out its natural oils, which gives a more intense chocolate flavor. You will see this come back in Chapter 7, when hot liquid is used in the chocolate cake recipe (page 149).

Salted Caramel Pecan Brownies (page 124)

Funfetti Blondies (page 128)

BLONDIE MASTER RECIPE

Yield: 9 large or 16 small bars
Specialty Equipment: 8-inch (20-cm) square baking pan
Mixing Method: The One-Bowl Method for Cookies
Prep Time: 20 minutes
Cook Time: 33 minutes
Total Time: 53 minutes

- 150 grams (¾ cup) brown sugar (preferably dark), lightly packed
- 50 grams (¼ cup) granulated sugar
- 113 grams (½ cup, 1 stick) unsalted butter, melted and slightly cooled
- 1 large egg, room temperature
- 1 egg yolk, room temperature
- 2 teaspoons vanilla
- ½ teaspoon baking powder
- 2 grams (½ teaspoon) kosher salt
- 160 grams (1⅓ cups) all-purpose flour

Blondies are the vanilla counterpart of brownies. Traditionally, they are made with add-ins that keep the "blonde" part of the name true, like white chocolate chips and/or walnuts. However, as with all of the other base recipes in this book, feel free to make them as you like! They are dense and chewy, with slightly crispy edges, and the perfect starting point for a cookie bar.

Method

Prep:

1. At least 30 minutes before baking, take the eggs out of the refrigerator to come to room temperature. Measure out the rest of the ingredients. Melt the butter and set aside to cool slightly.
2. Position an oven rack in the center position. Preheat the oven to 325°F/165°C.
3. Line an 8-inch (20-cm) square pan with parchment paper, or grease with non-stick spray.

To Make the Blondies:

1. In a large mixing bowl whisk together the brown sugar, granulated sugar, and melted butter.
2. Add the whole egg, egg yolk, and vanilla extract and whisk until well incorporated (about 30 seconds). If adding in any other extracts or zest, add those in here.
3. Add the baking powder, salt, flour, and any spices (if using) to the mixing bowl and use a silicone spatula or mixing spoon to stir together until well combined. Stir for about 30 seconds to purposely develop a little bit of gluten, which will give your blondies more chewiness. Fold in any solid mix-ins if using.
4. Transfer the mixture into your prepared pan and spread evenly.
5. Bake at 325°F/165°C for 28–33 minutes until a toothpick inserted in the center comes out clean.

6. Set the pan on a cooling rack to cool for at least 15 minutes to solidify before slicing.

7. Store leftover blondies at room temperature in an airtight container for 4–5 days.

Flavor Variation Ideas

♦ **Classic White Chocolate Walnut Blondies:** Add 150 grams (1 cup) white chocolate chips and 50 grams (½ cup) toasted (page 256), chopped walnuts to the batter.

♦ **Funfetti Blondies:** Add ½ teaspoon almond extract and 80 grams (½ cup) of rainbow sprinkles to the batter.

Flavoring Your Blondies

The base recipe does have a fairly strong vanilla flavor, so you may choose to reduce the amount of, or eliminate, the vanilla.

Extracts & Zests

(Use up to 2 additional extracts and/or zests, if desired)

- ½ teaspoon almond extract
- ¼ teaspoon anise extract
- 1 ½ teaspoons lemon, orange, or lime zest

Spices

(Use up to 1 ½ teaspoons total spices if desired)

- 1 teaspoon cinnamon
- 1 teaspoon ground ginger
- ¼ teaspoon cardamom
- ¼ teaspoon nutmeg
- ⅛ teaspoon cloves
- ⅛ teaspoon allspice
- 1 teaspoon apple pie spice
- 1 teaspoon pumpkin pie spice

Solid Mix-Ins

(Use up to 1 ½ cups total of solid mix-ins. You can use as many as you like within this volume. Recommended to only use up to 1 cup of any individual mix-in.)

- chips or chunks (semi-sweet, milk chocolate, bittersweet, dark chocolate, white chocolate, butterscotch, peanut butter)
- M&Ms (regular or mini)
- oats (old-fashioned or quick-cooking)
- nuts (pecans, almonds, pistachios, walnuts, macadamia nuts)
- dried fruit (cranberries, cherries, raisins, currants)

Baker Bettie's Better Baking Book

Classic White Chocolate Walnut Blondies (page 128)

The Creaming Method for Cookies

The Creaming Method is the most commonly used method for making cookies. It is used to make a wide variety of types, including chocolate chip cookies, oatmeal raisin cookies, and most other drop cookies. Shortbread and sugar cookies are also styles of cookies that utilize the Creaming Method.

The Creaming Method gets its name from the first step of the mixing process, where butter and sugar are creamed together. This process helps to lighten and leaven your cookies. Creaming butter and sugar together also increases the volume of your cookie dough, which means more cookies!

The Importance of Room Temperature Ingredients with the Creaming Method

As mentioned in Chapter 4, there are certain instances in which it is very important that your ingredients are at room temperature before starting. Creaming butter and sugar together is one of those instances.

When butter and sugar are beaten together, a web forms that traps air within it. This can only happen if the butter is at the proper temperature. It should be a cool room temperature—somewhere around 68–72°F/20–22°C. The butter should give some when you press on it, but it should not look greasy or runny.

Once your butter and sugar are properly creamed together, it is also important that other ingredients, such as eggs or milk, are also at room temperature, as it can break the creamed mixture if they are too cold.

What Does "Breaking" Mean in Baking?

A mixture "breaks" when an emulsion becomes unstable. Butter is an emulsion of fat and water, and when it is creamed with sugar, it incorporates the sugar and air into the emulsion. If other liquids are added too quickly or are too cold or too warm when added, the emulsion will become unstable and "break."

A broken mixture will look curdled and separated. This does not mean that it cannot be baked. But a cookie or cake baked from a broken batter will have a denser crumb and drier texture.

Creamed mixture   Broken mixture

Steps in the Creaming Method for Cookies

It is extremely important that the butter and eggs are completely at room temperature before mixing.

1. Beat the butter and sugar together on medium speed with an electric mixer. For dense and chewy cookies, cream for about 1 minute, and for fluffier cookies or to encourage more spreading, cream for 2–3 minutes.
2. Add the extracts, and then the eggs, one at a time, and beat on medium/low speed until incorporated before adding the next. It can cause your mixture to break if you add the eggs too fast.
3. Whisk together all of the dry ingredients in a separate bowl until well combined.
4. Add the dry ingredients into the creamed mixture and mix on medium/low speed until just incorporated.
5. Fold in mix-ins if using.
6. Transfer the dough to your prepared baking pan and bake.

Shortbread Tart Crust (page 136)

Shortbread Crumb Bars (page 136)

Shortbread Thumbprint Cookies (page 135)

Shortbread Cut-Out Cookies (page 134)

SHORTBREAD MASTER RECIPE

Specialty Equipment:

Hand mixer or stand mixer

Mixing Method: Creaming
Method for Cookies

- 113 grams (½ cup, 1 stick) unsalted butter, room temperature
- 50 grams (¼ cup) granulated sugar
- 1 gram (¼ teaspoon) kosher salt
- 128 grams (1 cup + 1 tablespoon) all-purpose flour

Shortbread is a simple dough made from very few ingredients. The flavor is buttery and rich and is delicious as is, or a variety of flavors can be added. Shortbread can be rolled out and cut into cookies, or used for cookie bars, as the base of a tart, or the crust of a cheesecake.

Method

Prep:

1. At least 30 minutes before mixing your dough, set out the butter to come to room temperature. Measure out the rest of the ingredients.

2. Prepare the oven and baking pan according to the specific use of the dough (details follow).

To Make the Shortbread Dough:

1. In the bowl of a stand mixer fitted with a paddle attachment, or in a large mixing bowl with a hand mixer, cream together the butter and sugar on medium speed until light and fluffy (about 2 minutes). Scrape down the sides and bottom of the bowl halfway through.

2. Add in the extracts and/or zest if using and mix until incorporated.

3. In a separate mixing bowl, whisk together the salt, flour, and any spices if using.

4. Add the flour mixture to the mixing bowl and mix on medium/low speed until just incorporated. The dough will likely be a bit crumbly-looking, but it should still look moist and hold together if pressed in your hand. If it does not, you can add about 1–2 tablespoons of milk or water until it holds together when pressed.

5. Shape and bake according to the specific application. This dough can be wrapped in plastic wrap and kept in the refrigerator for 3 days, or in the freezer for 3 months. Allow to soften before using.

Flavoring Your Shortbread

Use this chart of flavoring options as a guide for flavoring your dough if desired. Mix and match as you like.

Extracts & Zests

(Use 1–2 of these if desired)

- ½ teaspoon vanilla extract
- ¼ teaspoon almond extract
- ⅛ teaspoon anise extract
- 1 tablespoon lemon, lime, or orange zest

Spices

(Use up to 2 teaspoons total of combined spices, if desired)

- ½–1 teaspoon cinnamon
- ¼ teaspoon ginger
- ⅛ teaspoon nutmeg
- ⅛ teaspoon cardamom
- ⅛ teaspoon clove

Shortbread Cut-Out Cookies

Yield: About fourteen 2½-inch (6-cm) cookies

Prep + Chilling Time: 35 minutes

Cook Time: 16 minutes

Total Time: 51 minutes

1. Prepare a double batch of dough.

2. Turn it onto a clean work surface and gather it into one mass of dough, using gentle pressure to bring it together. Press it into a flat disk, about 1 inch (2.5 cm) thick.

3. Wrap in plastic wrap and refrigerate for 15 minutes to firm up.

4. Position oven racks in the top and bottom thirds of the oven. Preheat to 350°F/175°C. Line two sheet pans with parchment paper or silicone baking mats.

5. Lightly flour a clean work surface and place the chilled dough on it. Lightly flour the top of the dough and a rolling pin.

6. Roll the dough out to about ¼-inch thick. As you are rolling, rotate your dough on the work surface occasionally to check for sticking. Use more flour as needed to prevent sticking. When rolling dough, focus your pressure across the dough, rather than down into the table to help with sticking. If the dough cracks, use the warmth of your hands to press it back together.

7. Dip your cookie cutter(s) of choice in flour, stamp out the cookies, and transfer them to the prepared baking sheets, leaving about an inch between them. You may bring together your dough scraps and re-roll them, but keep in mind that the cookies will get tougher the more times you re-roll the dough.

8. As an optional step, sprinkle with granulated or coarse sugar if you will not be icing. You can also use a fork to dock each cookie for a classic shortbread look.

9. Bake for 12–16 minutes until golden brown, rotating the pans halfway through baking from top to bottom and front to back.

10. Allow to cool on the baking sheets for 5 minutes before removing and transferring to a cooling rack to cool completely. These cookies are delicious on their own, but they can also be iced with American buttercream (page 175) or cream cheese frosting (page 177).

11. Store cooled cookies in an airtight container at room temperature for up to 2 weeks.

Shortbread Thumbprint Cookies

Yield: 18–22 cookies
Prep: 20 minutes
Cook Time: 16 minutes
Total Time: 36 minutes

1. Position oven racks in the top and bottom thirds of the oven. Preheat the oven to 350°F/175°C. Line two baking sheets with parchment paper or silicone baking mats.

2. Prepare the dough with ¼ teaspoon of almond extract.

3. Scoop the dough into 1-tablespoon portions, roll into a smooth ball between the palms of your hands, and then roll in granulated sugar.

4. Place the balls of dough on the prepared baking sheets and press your thumb into the top of each, going about ½-inch (1-cm) deep.

5. Spoon about ½ teaspoon of your jam of choice into each thumbprint.

6. Place the tray in the freezer for about 10 minutes before baking. This helps them not spread out in the oven.

7. Bake at 350°F/175°C for 12–16 minutes, until set and very lightly browned on the bottoms. They will stay very pale.

8. Cool for about 5 minutes on the baking sheets before moving to a cooling rack to cool completely.

9. Optional: Drizzle cooled cookies with powdered sugar glaze (page 257).

Shortbread Crumb Bars

Yield: 9 bars
Prep Time: 20 minutes
Cook Time: 30 minutes
Total Time: 50 minutes

1. Position an oven rack in the center position. Preheat the oven to 350°F/175°C. Prepare an 8-inch (20-cm) square baking pan with parchment or non-stick spray.
2. Make the dough. Divide out about 75 grams (½ cup) of the dough and set aside. Press the remaining dough evenly into the prepared pan.
3. Spread 140 grams (½ cup) jam of choice over the top of the dough.
4. Crumble the remaining shortbread dough over the top of the jam. If desired, sprinkle 25 grams (¼ cup) chopped nuts of choice evenly over the top. No need to toast the nuts first, as they will toast in the oven.
5. Bake at 350°F/175°C for 26–30 minutes, until the center is set.
6. Set the pan on a cooling rack for at least 15 minutes.
7. If desired, drizzle with a powdered sugar glaze (page 257) before slicing.
8. Cut into 9 bars. Store leftover bars, wrapped in foil or plastic wrap, at room temperature for up to 4 days.

Shortbread Tart or Pie Crust

Yield: Crust for a 9-inch (23-cm) round, or a 14 x 4-inch (36 x 10-cm) tart or
pie pan, double the amounts for a 9 x 13-inch (23 x 33-cm) pan.
Prep Time: 20 minutes
Cook Time: 15 minutes for parbaked/20 minutes for fully baked
Total Time: 35 minutes for parbaked/40 minutes for fully baked

1. Position an oven rack in the center. Preheat the oven to 350°F/175°C.
2. Make the dough, then press it into a 9-inch (23-cm) round tart, pie, or springform pan, or a 14 x 4-inch (36 x 10-cm) tart pan. If using a pie plate, only go about 1 inch (2.5 cm) up the side.
3. Dock the crust with a fork to prevent it from puffing up while baking.
4. **If the filling will also need to be baked**, bake the crust by itself at 350°F/175°C for 14–15 minutes, until the edges are lightly browned, before adding the filling. The filling can be added while the crust is still warm if it will also be baked.
5. **If the filling will not need to be baked**, bake the crust for 16–20 minutes until it is completely golden brown and a toothpick comes out clean from the center. Allow the crust to cool completely on a cooling rack before adding the filling.

Chewy Chocolate Chip Pecan Cookies (page 140) and Spiced Rum-Soaked Oatmeal Raisin Cookies (page 140)

DROP COOKIE MASTER RECIPE

Yield: About sixteen 2-inch (5-cm) cookies

Specialty Equipment:
Hand mixer or stand mixer

Mixing Method: Creaming Method for Cookies

Prep Time: 20 minutes

Cook Time: 10 minutes

Total Time: 30 minutes

- 50 grams (¼ cup) granulated sugar
- 100 grams (½ cup) brown sugar, light or dark
- 113 grams (½ cup, 1 stick) unsalted butter, room temperature
- 1½ teaspoons vanilla
- 1 large egg, room temperature
- 2 grams (½ teaspoon) kosher salt
- ¼ teaspoon baking soda
- ½ teaspoon baking powder
- 135 grams (1 cup + 2 tablespoons) all-purpose flour

This base recipe for drop cookies can be used for a standard chocolate chip cookie, or for a wide variety of variations. Use the list of flavorings and mix-ins to get creative and make your favorite flavor! The recipe as written creates a cookie that isn't too thick or thin, with slightly crispy edges and a soft and chewy middle. See the note section about how to change the texture.

Method

Prep:

1. At least 30 minutes before making your cookies, set out the butter and egg to come to room temperature.

2. Position two oven racks in the top third and the bottom third of the oven. Preheat the oven to 375°F/190°C.

3. Measure out the rest of the ingredients. Line 2 baking sheets with parchment paper or a silicone baking mat.

To Make the Cookies:

1. In the bowl of a stand mixer fitted with a paddle attachment, or a large mixing bowl with a hand mixer, cream the butter with the granulated sugar and brown sugar on medium/high speed. Cream for about 2 minutes, until light and fluffy, scraping down the bowl periodically.

2. Add the vanilla, the egg, and any other extracts or zests if using, and mix on medium speed until combined.

3. Whisk together the flour, salt, baking soda, baking powder, and any spices if using, in a separate mixing bowl.

4. Add the flour mixture to the butter mixture and mix on medium/low speed until just incorporated, scraping the bowl as needed.

5. Fold in the solid mix-ins until just combined.

6. Scoop rounded mounds of dough, about 2 tablespoons each, onto baking sheets lined with parchment paper or a silicone baking mat. It is best to only scoop about 8 cookies per sheet to allow enough room for

spreading. ***A tip for making picture-perfect cookies***: top each mound of dough with a few of the solid add-ins you choose so that they are visible after baked.

7. Bake two cookie sheets at a time at 375°F/190°C for 7–10 minutes, rotating the pans from top to bottom halfway through. Remove the cookies from the oven when the edges are lightly browned and the cookies look slightly underbaked in the center. They will continue cooking after they are removed from the oven.

8. Allow the cookies to cool on the baking sheets for 5 minutes before moving them to cooling racks to cool completely.

9. Store cookies in an airtight container for up to 1 week at room temperature. Alternatively, you can freeze the cookies for up to 3 months.

Flavor Variation Ideas

♦ **Monster Cookies:** Reduce the butter to 56 grams (½ stick) and add 64 grams (¼ cup) of creamy peanut butter. Cream the peanut butter together with the butter and sugar. Add 50 grams (½ cup) rolled oats, 85 grams (½ cup) M&Ms, and 75 grams (½ cup) chocolate chips to the dough.

♦ **Spiced Rum-Soaked Oatmeal Raisin Cookies:** Soak 150 grams (1 cup) raisins in enough spiced rum to cover for at least 4 hours and up to 12 hours. Drain well. Add 1 teaspoon cinnamon to the dry ingredients, and add the drained raisins and 100 grams (1 cup) rolled oats to the dough. Sprinkle with flaky salt when they come out of the oven.

♦ **Chewy Chocolate Chip Pecan Cookies:** Melt the butter and allow to cool slightly, but not until solidified. Use the One-Bowl Method to mix your dough. Add 150 grams (1 cup) bittersweet or dark chocolate chips (my favorite are Ghirardelli 60 percent bittersweet chips), and 75 grams (¾ cup) toasted (page 256), chopped pecans to your dough. Sprinkle with flaky salt when they come out of the oven.

How to Alter the Texture of Your Drop Cookies:

• **For a crispier texture:** Substitute half of the brown sugar with more granulated sugar. Increase the baking time by 1–2 minutes.

• **For a softer texture:** Substitute all of the granulated sugar with more brown sugar.

• **To make a really chewy cookie:** Melt the butter and use the One-Bowl Method instead of the Creaming Method.

• **To make thick cookies that don't spread much:** Place the scooped cookies in the freezer for 10–15 minutes before baking. Increase baking time by 1–2 minutes.

• **To make thinner cookies that spread a lot:** Cream the butter and sugar for 3 full minutes. Decrease the baking temperature to 325°F/165°C and increase the baking time to 16–18 minutes.

Baker Bettie's Better Baking Book

Flavoring Your Drop Cookies

Use this chart of flavoring options as a guide for flavoring your dough if desired. Mix and match as you like.

Extracts & Zests

(Use up to 2 extracts and/or zests if desired)

- ½ teaspoon anise extract
- ¼ teaspoon almond extract
- 1 tablespoon orange, lemon, or lime zest

Spices

(Use up to 1½ teaspoons total spices if desired)

- 1 teaspoon cinnamon
- 1 teaspoon ground ginger
- ½ teaspoon cardamom
- ½ teaspoon nutmeg
- ⅛ teaspoon cloves
- ⅛ teaspoon allspice
- 1 teaspoon apple pie spice
- 1 teaspoon pumpkin pie spice

Cocoa Powder

To add cocoa powder to your cookie dough, reduce the amount of flour to 120 grams (1 cup) and add 10 grams (2 tablespoons) cocoa powder (Dutch-processed or natural) to your dry ingredients.

Solid Mix-Ins

(Use up to 2½ cups total solid mix-ins. You can use as many as you like within this volume. Recommended to only use up to 1 cup of any individual mix-in)

- chips or chunks (semi-sweet, milk chocolate, bittersweet, dark chocolate, white chocolate, butterscotch, peanut butter)
- M&Ms (regular or mini)
- nuts (pecans, almonds, pistachios, walnuts, macadamia nuts)
- dried fruit (cranberries, cherries, raisins, currants)
- oats (quick-cooking or rolled oats) *(Note: Oats will add a chewier texture to the cookies and the cookies won't spread as much)*

Peanut Butter

To add peanut butter to your dough, reduce the butter to 56 grams (½ stick) and add 64 grams (¼ cup) peanut butter. Cream the peanut butter together with the butter and sugar.

Marble Pound Cake (page 156) with Ganache Glaze (page 253)

7

Cakes

Cakes were one of the last things that I learned to perfect when I first started baking. Something about them felt very fussy and intimidating. But truthfully, this was only because I didn't understand cake mixing methods.

While the mixing methods we have learned up to this point have been important for getting your desired results, I cannot emphasize enough how important they are for making cakes. In order to achieve cakes that are tall, fluffy, and moist, executing mixing methods properly is essential.

Cake Mixing Methods

As discussed in the cookie chapter, there are two cake mixing methods that sort of correspond with the cookie mixing methods we covered: The One-Bowl Method for Cakes (also known as the Blending Method) and the Creaming Method for Cakes. Most basic cakes are made using one of these two methods.

There is also a category of mixing methods in cake making called foaming or sponge methods. These titles are general terms for a variety of methods that rely on whipping air into eggs (either whole or separated) to help leaven the cake. The process by which the air is whipped into the eggs varies depending on the variety of cake.

Using Cake Flour in Cakes

Many of the cake recipes in this book will call for cake flour. Cake flour is a specialty type of flour that has been bleached and finely milled. Bleaching weakens the protein in the flour, which means it cannot create a strong gluten structure. Using cake flour can result in cakes that are extremely light and tender.

If you are unable to find cake flour, you can make a substitute by mixing all-purpose flour with cornstarch and sifting it thoroughly. See page 49 for the exact ratios.

Preparing Pans for Cake Baking

One of the most important parts of the cake making process is preparing your pans so that your cake will release easily.

For cupcakes, I recommend using paper cupcake liners. While you can simply grease your cupcake tins, liners provide a much easier way to serve and transport your cupcakes.

If you will be turning your cake out of the pans, as with a layer cake for instance, I recommend spraying your pans very well with non-stick spray and then lining the bottoms with parchment paper. This will ensure that the cake releases easily and doesn't stick to the bottom of the pan.

To Create a Parchment Round for Your Cake Pan:

1. Start with a square piece of parchment paper that is slightly bigger than your cake pan.
2. Fold it in half, bringing the bottom to the top.
3. Next, fold the parchment in half again, this time bringing the left side to the right side.
4. Fold the parchment into a thin triangle by bringing the right side to the left side and then repeating that fold one more time.
5. Measure your parchment by placing the point of the triangle in the center of your pan. Cut the parchment right at the edge of the pan.
6. Unfold the paper to reveal your parchment circle.

For specialty pans with intricate details, like a Bundt pan, make sure you spray it extremely well with non-stick spray, getting into all of the nooks and crannies. I like to use a baking spray that has flour mixed into it for an extra insurance policy. If you only have regular non-stick spray, you can also dust your pan with a bit of flour (or cocoa powder for chocolate cakes) and tap it around the inside of the pan after spraying it.

It is also important to note that typically you will not want to grease a tube pan at all. Cakes baked in this pan, like angel food cake, typically rely on the ability to cling to and climb the walls and center tube of the pan.

The Blending Method

The Blending Method (also referred to as the "One-Bowl Method") relies on chemical leavening and the liquid in the recipe to make the cake rise. This produces a cake with an incredibly tender texture and a bit of a denser crumb than cakes made with the Creaming Method.

The purpose of this method is to coat the flour and the rest of the ingredients with fat before the liquid is added. As we've discussed previously, fat serves as a barrier between the flour and liquid, which inhibits gluten formation. Liquid fat is typically used for this method, which creates a cake that stays moister and more tender than cakes made with solid fat. Cakes made with this method do not typically work well as large multi-tiered cakes because they are so tender.

Steps of the Blending Method for Cakes

Make sure all ingredients are at room temperature before beginning.

1. Sift all of the dry ingredients.
2. Combine the dry ingredients and fat in a mixing bowl. Use a hand mixer or stand mixer to combine for about 1 minute.
3. Add the eggs and any extracts.
4. Slowly add in the rest of the liquid with the mixer running on medium speed.
5. Finish mixing for about 1 minute to thoroughly combine.
6. Transfer to the prepared pan(s) and bake.

Crumb Cake (page 156)

Chocolate Sheet Cake with Chocolate Buttercream (page 176)

CLASSIC CHOCOLATE CAKE MASTER RECIPE

Yield: One 9 x 13-inch (23 x 33-cm) sheet cake, or two 9-inch (23-cm) round layer cakes, or three 8-inch (20-cm) round layer cakes, or about 24 cupcakes

Specialty Equipment: Either a 9 x 13-inch (23 x 33-cm) pan, three 8-inch (20-cm) round cake pans, two 9-inch (23-cm) round cake pans, or two 12 cup muffin/cupcake tins

Mixing Method:
Blending Method

Prep Time: 20 minutes

Cook Time: 45 minutes for sheet cake/30 minutes for cake layers/25 minutes for cupcakes

Total Time: 1 hour 5 minutes for sheet cake/50 minutes for cake layers/45 minutes for cupcakes

- 240 grams (2 cups) all-purpose flour
- 100 grams (1¼ cups) natural cocoa powder
- 450 grams (2¼ cups) granulated sugar
- 7 grams (2 teaspoons) baking powder
- 4 grams (1 teaspoon) baking soda

Continued on next page

This is my all-time favorite chocolate cake recipe. It is incredibly simple to make and always receives rave reviews. The coffee in the recipe isn't overpowering and actually enhances the chocolate flavor. However, you can reduce the amount of coffee and substitute some or all of it with hot water. This cake is extremely moist and tender, and therefore I use all-purpose flour rather than cake flour to give it more structure.

Method

Prep:

1. At least 30 minutes before making the cake, take the eggs out of the refrigerator and measure out the milk to come to room temperature.
2. Position the oven rack to the center position. Preheat the oven to 350°F/175°C. Prepare your baking pan with non-stick spray and parchment paper, or with paper liners if making cupcakes.
3. Measure out the rest of the ingredients. The coffee or water should be very hot when you mix the cake.

To Make the Cake:

1. In a large mixing bowl, or the bowl of a stand mixer, sift together the flour, cocoa powder, granulated sugar, baking powder, and baking soda. Add the salt and whisk to evenly distribute.
2. Add the oil into the mixing bowl and mix on medium/low speed with a hand mixer, or a stand mixer fitted with the paddle attachment, for about 1 minute, until well combined.
3. Add the eggs and vanilla extract to the bowl and mix on medium/low speed until all incorporated.
4. With the mixer still running, slowly pour in the milk and then the hot coffee or water.

- 3 grams (¾ teaspoon) fine sea salt
- 170 grams (¾ cup, 180 milliliters) neutral oil (canola, vegetable, safflower, or grapeseed)
- 3 large eggs, room temperature
- 1 tablespoon vanilla extract
- 151 grams (⅔ cup, 160 milliliters) milk, room temperature (1 percent, 2 percent, or whole)
- 340 grams (1½ cups, 360 milliliters) very hot coffee or water

5. Continue mixing until everything is evenly incorporated (about 1 minute). This is a very thin batter. Scrape down the sides and bottom of the bowl.

6. Pour the batter into the prepared pan(s). If making cupcakes, leave about ½-inch space at the tops.

7. Bake at 350°F/175°C. A sheet cake will take about 35–45 minutes. Layer cakes will take 25–30 minutes, and cupcakes will take 18–25 minutes. Pull out of the oven when the cake is firm but springs back when gently pressed in the center, or when a cake tester comes out clean.

8. Cool the cakes in their pans completely on a cooling rack before turning out of the pan and frosting.

9. Store the cake covered in foil or plastic wrap, at room temperature, for up to 3 days.

Flavor Variation Idea

♦ **Death by Chocolate Cake:** Frost with whipped ganache frosting (page 253). Top with mini chocolate chips or chocolate shavings.

Baking Science Note: Natural cocoa powder is the acidic ingredient needed to activate the baking soda. If you do not have natural cocoa powder, you can use Dutch-processed cocoa powder, but omit the baking soda and increase the baking powder to 10 grams (1 tablespoon).

Chocolate Cupcakes (page 149) with Peanut Butter Buttercream (page 176)

The Creaming Method for Cakes

The Creaming Method for Cakes starts out with the same concepts as the Creaming Method for Cookies. The ingredients need to be at room temperature so that the butter and sugar can be properly creamed together.

Where this method deviates is that cakes require much more liquid than cookies do, and you need to be careful about how you add the liquid into the batter. If you add the liquid in too quickly, the creamed mixture might break, resulting in a denser cake. Therefore, the method calls for alternating adding in part of the dry ingredients with part of the liquid until it is all combined. Typically, this is done with three stages of dry ingredients and two stages of liquid ingredients, starting and ending with the dry ingredients.

Cakes made with the Creaming Method tend to be a bit sturdier while still being very tender and moist. The rich buttery flavor is desired in a cake made with the Creaming Method; however, these cakes do not stay moist for as long as oil-based cakes do.

Steps of the Creaming Method for Cakes

It is extremely important that all ingredients are at room temperature before starting. Depending on the temperature of your kitchen, you may need more than the "at least 30 minutes" stated in the recipe to allow the ingredients to come to room temperature.

1. Sift all of the dry ingredients.
2. Cream together the butter and sugar until very light and fluffy, about 5 minutes at medium speed.
3. Add any extracts, and then add the eggs in one at a time, mixing until completely absorbed before adding the next egg to avoid breaking the mixture.
4. Alternate adding the dry ingredients in with the wet ingredients in stages, starting and ending with the dry ingredients.
5. Add the dry ingredients in three additions and the wet ingredients in two additions.
6. Transfer to the prepared pan(s) and bake.

POUND CAKE MASTER RECIPE

Yield: 1 Loaf

Specialty Equipment: Stand mixer or hand mixer, 8.5-inch x 4.5-inch (22 x 11-cm) loaf pan

Mixing Method Utilized: Creaming Method for Cakes

Prep Time: 25 minutes

Cook Time: 65 minutes

Total Time: 1 hour 30 minutes

- 215 grams (2 cups minus 2 tablespoons) cake flour
- ¼ teaspoon fine sea salt
- 226 grams (1 cup, 2 sticks) unsalted butter, room temperature
- 300 grams (1 ½ cups) granulated sugar
- 1 teaspoon vanilla extract
- 4 large eggs, room temperature
- 60 grams (¼ cup) sour cream, room temperature

This classic pound cake is buttery and rich, with a very tight crumb structure. The simple flavor of butter and vanilla is an excellent canvas to pair with fresh berries and a dollop of whipped cream. Or use this as your go-to base recipe for creating endless flavors. The original pound cake got its name from the recipe that called for only a pound of butter, a pound of sugar, a pound of eggs, and a pound of flour. My version changes those ratios slightly and adds some sour cream for a cake that is a bit more moist.

Method

Prep:

1. At least 30 minutes before mixing the batter, take the butter, eggs, and sour cream out of the refrigerator to come to room temperature. *It is especially important that the eggs are room temperature for this recipe due to the large quantity.* Measure out the rest of the ingredients.

2. Position an oven rack to the center position. Preheat the oven to 350°F/175°C.

3. Prepare your loaf pan with non-stick spray and parchment paper.

To Make the Cake Batter:

1. Sift the cake flour, and any additional spices if using. Add the salt, whisk together, and set aside.

2. In the bowl of a stand mixer fitted with the paddle attachment, or in a large bowl with a hand mixer, combine the butter and sugar. Cream together on medium speed until very light and fluffy, about 5 minutes. Stop the mixer and scrape down the sides of the bowl several times during mixing. The mixture should be very pale yellow after mixing.

3. With the mixer running, add the vanilla. Next, add in one egg at a time, mixing on medium speed and allowing each egg to fully incorporate before adding the next. Scrape down the sides of the bowl frequently. Do not rush this process.

4. If you are adding any fruit juice or zests to your batter, mix them with your sour cream here. Alternate adding the dry ingredients into the bowl in three additions with the sour cream in two additions, starting and ending with the dry ingredients. Mix on medium speed between additions until fully incorporated.

5. If you are adding any solid mix-ins, fold them into the batter here.

6. Transfer the batter into your prepared pan and bake at 350°F/175°C for 55–65 minutes until a cake tester inserted into the middle of the cake comes out with moist crumbs.

7. Set the pan(s) on a cooling rack and allow the cake to cool for 20 minutes before turning out of the pan to fully cool.

8. Wrap leftover cake in plastic wrap when fully cooled and keep at room temperature for up to 3 days.

Flavor Variation Ideas

♦ **Marble Pound Cake:** Divide the batter in half and stir 10 grams (2 tablespoons) cocoa powder into one-half of the batter. Spoon each batter into the pan, alternating between plain and chocolate. Use a butter knife to swirl the batter to make a marble pattern. Top with chocolate ganache glaze (page 253).

♦ **Crumb Cake:** Transfer the batter to a greased 9 x 13-inch (23 x 33-cm) pan. Top with a double batch of streusel topping (page 261). Bake for 45–55 minutes until a cake tester comes out with moist crumbs.

To Make into a Bundt Cake: Prepare a 12-cup Bundt pan or a 10-inch (25-cm) tube pan with non-stick spray. Add a few tablespoons of flour to the pan and tap it all around, dumping out any excess. Make a double batch of the batter (note, this will be a very large quantity and will require a mixing bowl at least 5 quarts in size). Bake at 350°F/175°C for 1 hour 10 minutes to 1 hour 20 minutes, until a cake tester inserted into the middle of the cake comes out with moist crumbs.

Flavoring Your Pound Cake

You can flavor your pound cake in a variety of ways by adding spices, extracts, and solid mix-ins.

Extracts & Zests

(Use 1–2 extracts or zest if desired)

- 1 teaspoon almond extract
- ½ teaspoon anise extract
- 3 tablespoons lemon, lime, or orange zest + 3 tablespoons lemon, lime, or orange juice

Spices

(Use up to 3 teaspoons total combined spices if desired. Choose as many as you like within this volume.)

- 2 teaspoons cinnamon
- 1 teaspoon ginger
- ½ teaspoon nutmeg
- ½ teaspoon cardamom
- ¼ teaspoon clove
- ¼ teaspoon allspice

Solid Mix-Ins

(Use up to 2 cups total of solid mix-ins if desired. Choose as many as you like within this volume.)

- chocolate chips or chunks (milk chocolate, semi-sweet, dark, or white)
- chopped nuts (walnuts, pecans, almonds, pistachios)
- dried fruit (cranberries, cherries, raisins, currants)
- poppy seeds (only up to ¼ cup)
- shredded coconut

Funfetti Cake (page 160) with Vanilla Buttercream (page 175)

CLASSIC WHITE CAKE

Yield: One 9 x 13-inch (23 x 33-cm) sheet cake, two 9-inch (23-cm) round layer cakes, three 8-inch (20-cm) layer cakes, or about 24 cupcakes

Specialty Equipment: Either a 9 x 13-inch (23 x 33-cm) pan, three 8-inch (20-cm) round cake pans, two 9-inch (23-cm) round cake pans, or two 12 cup muffin/cupcake tins

Mixing Method Utilized: Creaming Method for Cakes

Prep Time: 25 minutes

Cook Time: 45 minutes for sheet cake/26 minutes for cake layers/25 minutes for cupcakes

Total Time: 1 hour 10 minutes for sheet cake/51 minutes for cake layers/50 minutes for cupcakes

- 345 grams (3 cups) cake flour
- 7 grams (2 teaspoons) baking powder
- ½ teaspoon baking soda
- 2 grams (½ teaspoon) fine sea salt
- 226 grams (8 ounces, 2 sticks) unsalted butter, softened
- 400 grams (2 cups) granulated sugar
- 2 teaspoons vanilla extract

Continued on next page

White cake keeps its pale color by only utilizing egg whites instead of whole eggs. Some recipes call for these egg whites to be whipped into a meringue and folded into the batter (Foaming Method); however, I prefer using the Creaming Method for this cake, as I find it produces the perfect balance of cake that is moist and fluffy.

Method

Prep:

1. At least 30 minutes before mixing, take the butter, eggs, milk, and sour cream out of the refrigerator to come to room temperature. Separate the eggs. Measure out the rest of the ingredients.

2. Position the oven rack to the center position. Preheat the oven to 350°F/175°C. Prepare your baking pan(s) with non-stick spray and parchment paper, or with paper liners if making cupcakes.

To Make into a Bundt Cake:

1. Sift together the cake flour, baking powder, and baking soda. Add the salt, whisk together, and set aside.

2. In the bowl of a stand mixer fitted with the paddle attachment, or in a large bowl with a hand mixer, combine the butter and sugar. Cream together on medium speed until very light and fluffy, about 5 minutes. Stop the mixer and scrape down the sides and bottom of the bowl halfway through mixing. The mixture should be very pale yellow after mixing.

3. With the mixer running on medium/low speed, add the vanilla and almond extracts. Next, slowly add in the egg whites while the mixer continues running. Scrape down the sides of the bowl periodically as you slowly incorporate the egg whites.

4. Mix the milk and sour cream together. Alternate adding the dry ingredients into the bowl in three additions with the milk/sour cream mixture in two additions, starting and ending with the dry ingredients. Mix on medium speed between additions until fully incorporated.

- 1 teaspoon almond extract
- 160 grams (about 5 large, ⅔ cup) egg whites
- 180 grams (¾ cup) sour cream
- 170 grams (¾ cup, 180 milliliters) whole milk

5. Transfer the batter into the prepared pan(s). Bake at 350°F/175°C. A sheet cake will take about 35–45 minutes. Layer cakes will take 22–26 minutes, and cupcakes will take 18–25 minutes. Pull out of the oven when the cake is firm but springs back when gently pressed in on the center, or when a cake tester comes out clean.

6. Cool the cakes in their pan completely on a cooling rack before turning out of the pan and frosting.

7. Store the cake covered in foil or plastic wrap at room temperature for up to 3 days.

Flavor Variation Ideas

♦ **Funfetti Cake:** Increase the vanilla to 1 tablespoon and fold in 80 grams (½ cup) of rainbow sprinkles at the end. Pair with vanilla buttercream frosting (page 175).

♦ **Coconut Cake:** Replace the almond extract with 1 teaspoon coconut extract and the milk with canned coconut milk. Fold in 80 grams (1 cup) shredded sweetened coconut at the end. Pair with coconut cream cheese frosting (page 177). Top with additional shredded coconut if desired.

Coconut Cake (page 160)

Foaming Methods

Cake mixing methods can start becoming a bit more confusing once we dive into foaming methods. The reason for this is that there are several different types of foaming methods, each with its own process. In this book, we are addressing the methods that utilize whipping air into only the egg whites as the foaming component: the Angel Food Method and the Chiffon Mixing Method.

Tips for Properly Foaming Egg Whites

Creating an egg white foam is a fairly simple skill, but there are a few things that need to be kept in mind. Here are a few rules of thumb for properly foaming egg whites:

- **Make sure there is no fat present.** Fat inhibits the foaming of egg whites. Take extra caution that you do not get any yolk into your whites and that your tools are grease-free.
- **Room temperature whites foam more easily and beat to a higher volume.** Allow your eggs to fully come to room temperature before beating them.
- **Acidic ingredients and sugar help stabilize the egg foam.** Recipes often call for adding a bit of cream of tartar, lemon juice, or white vinegar into the egg whites to help stabilize them. It is also important that the sugar is added in very slowly and only *after the egg whites are already starting to hold soft peaks.* This helps keep the meringue stable.
- **Slower mixing creates a more stable meringue.** I recommend mixing your egg whites at medium speed and not rushing the process. Beating the egg whites at high speed will cause them to foam more quickly, but they will be less stable and not hold the air as well.

The Angel Food Method

The Angel Food Method is a mixing method used specifically for angel food cake, and it utilizes an egg white foam as the main structure of the cake.

This method calls for flour to be gently folded into a simple meringue and then baked. The result is an incredibly tender cake that has an almost cloud-like texture. It also stays very moist despite the fact that there is no fat present. This is due to the sugar content in this cake.

The Angel Food Method Process

Make sure the egg whites are at room temperature before beginning.

1. Reserve half of the sugar for the egg whites. Sift the rest of the dry ingredients together.

2. Whip the egg whites on medium speed until foamy. Add the acidic ingredient and continue whipping until they are starting to hold soft peaks.

3. Slowly add in the other half of the sugar while continuing to mix. Stop mixing when you reach stiff peaks and the foam looks glossy.

4. Gently fold the dry ingredients into your meringue, taking care not to deflate it.

5. Transfer the batter to the pan and bake. Angel food cake is traditionally baked in a tube pan, but it can be baked into cupcakes or a layer cake as well.

6. If you baked your cake in a tube pan, allow it to cool fully upside down. This helps the cake to not fall as it cools.

Angel Food Cake with Strawberry Sauce (page 250) and Whipped Cream (page 263)

ANGEL FOOD CAKE RECIPE

Yield: 1 tube cake, 22–24 cupcakes, one 8-inch (20-cm) 3-layer cake, or one 9-inch (23-cm) 2-layer cake

Specialty Equipment: Hand mixer or stand mixer; either a tube pan, three 8-inch (20-cm) round cake pans, two 9-inch (23-cm) round cake pans, or two 12-cup cupcake pans

Mixing Method:
Angel Food Method

Prep Time: 25 minutes

Cook Time: 22 minutes for cupcakes and layers/35 minutes for tube pan

Total Time: 47 minutes for cupcakes and layers/1 hour for tube pan

- 300 grams (1 ½ cups) granulated sugar
- 115 grams (1 cup) cake flour
- ¼ teaspoon fine sea salt
- 300 grams (1 ¼ cup, 295 milliliters) egg whites, room temperature (from about 9 or 10 large eggs)
- 1 ½ teaspoons cream of tartar (or lemon juice)
- 1 teaspoon lemon zest (optional but recommended)

Angel food cake is one of the simplest cakes to make. It is incredibly light and tender, as it is essentially just baked meringue with some cake flour folded in.

Method

Prep:

1. At least 30 minutes before baking, take the eggs out of the refrigerator and separate out the whites. Allow to come to room temperature.
2. Position an oven rack to the center position. If making cupcakes, position oven racks in the top and bottom third of the oven. Preheat the oven to 350°F/175°C.
3. If using a tube pan (which is traditional for angel food cake), do not grease it. Alternatively, prepare three 8-inch (20-cm) or two 9-inch (23-cm) round cake pans by greasing them and lining the bottoms with parchment paper. For cupcakes, line two 12-cup muffin pans with cupcake liners
4. Measure out the rest of the ingredients. Divide the sugar into two roughly equal portions.

To Make the Cake:

1. In a medium bowl, sift together the cake flour and half of the sugar. Add the salt and whisk together to evenly incorporate.
2. Place all of the egg whites in the bowl of a stand mixer fitted with a whisk attachment, or in a large bowl with a hand mixer. Beat on medium speed until the whites are starting to look frothy. Add the cream of tartar (or lemon juice) and continue beating on medium speed until the eggs are holding soft peaks.
3. Start adding the other half of the sugar to the egg whites about one tablespoon at a time, while beating at medium speed. Do not rush this process, as doing it slowly will help create a very stable meringue. Once all the sugar is added, you can add the lemon zest if using. Increase the speed to medium/high and whip to stiff peaks. They should look glossy and stand tall.

4. Lightly sprinkle the dry ingredients over the egg whites. Using a silicone spatula, begin folding the dry ingredients into the egg whites. This should only take about 20–30 seconds. Be gentle so that you do not deflate the whites.

5. Gently transfer the batter into the pan(s). For cupcakes, leave only about ¼-inch (½-cm) from the top. Bake at 350°F/175°C for 30–35 minutes for a tube pan and 18–22 minutes for layer cakes or cupcakes. *Do not open the oven during the first 15 minutes of baking, or the cake may fall.* If baking 2 trays of cupcakes, rotate them after the first 15 minutes. The cake is finished when browned and dry to the touch and the top springs back when gently pressed.

6. If you baked in a tube pan, carefully invert the pan and set it upside down onto a bottle (with the neck through the center) and place it on a stable surface to cool for 1 ½ hours. This will help it hold its height. Once the cake is completely cooled, turn right-side-up and remove it from the pan by running a butter knife around the sides and the bottom. **If you baked layer cakes or cupcakes**, set the pans on a cooling rack until completely cool.

7. Angel food cake is typically served with fresh berries and whipped cream (page 263). Berry sauce (page 250) is also delicious with this cake.

8. To store, wrap the completely cooled cake well with plastic wrap and keep in the refrigerator for 4–5 days.

 Note: Like all sponge cakes, it will taste eggy if served while still warm. Allow the cake to cool completely before serving.

Flavor Variation Idea

♦ **Chocolate Angel Food Cake:** Reduce the cake flour to 86 grams (¾ cup) and add 20 grams (¼ cup) cocoa powder (natural or Dutch-processed). Sift it in with the dry ingredients.

Chocolate Angel Food Cake (page 166) with Chocolate Ganache Glaze (page 253)

The Chiffon Mixing Method

Chiffon cakes are among my favorites. While this mixing method does take a little more effort than other mixing methods, the final result is worth it. Chiffon cakes are different from other foam cakes because they include a decent amount of fat, whereas most foam cakes contain little or no fat. This creates a cake that is very light and fluffy, while still being moist and rich.

The Chiffon Method calls for mixing the ingredients in three parts—dry ingredients, wet ingredients, and egg foam—and then combining them all together. It is extremely important to take extra care when folding the egg whites into the batter. Take your time and be patient in order to preserve as much air in the whites as possible.

Steps in the Chiffon Mixing Method

Mise en place is extra important with this method. Have all ingredients at room temperature before starting.

1. Sift together the dry ingredients.
2. Whisk all of the wet ingredients together until well combined.
3. Whisk the egg whites until they are starting to hold soft peaks.
4. Very slowly stream in the reserved sugar while continuing to mix on medium speed. Once all of the sugar is added, continue mixing until you reach stiff peaks.
5. Pour the wet ingredients into the dry ingredients and stir with a spatula or mixing spoon until well combined.
6. Add about a quarter of the egg whites to the batter and stir them in completely to loosen up the batter slightly.
7. Add about half of what is left of the egg whites and gently fold them into the batter, cutting down through the center and bringing the batter from the bottom of the bowl up to the top, rotating 90 degrees each time.
8. Continue doing this until the first half of the egg whites are mostly folded in. Then continue with the rest of the whites. You want to preserve as much air as possible in the whites.
9. Transfer to the prepared pan(s) and bake.

Yellow Cupcakes with Whipped Ganache Frosting (page 253)

YELLOW CHIFFON CAKE RECIPE

Yield: Either a 9 x 13-inch (23 x 33-cm) sheet cake, an 8-inch (20-cm) 3-layer cake, a 9-inch (23-cm) 2-layer cake, 24 cupcakes, or 1 tube cake

Specialty Equipment: Stand mixer or hand mixer; either a 9 x 13-inch (23 x 33-cm) pan, three 8-inch (20-cm) round cake pans, two 9-inch (23-cm) round cake pans, two 12-cup muffin/cupcake tins, or 1 tube pan

Mixing Method Utilized: Chiffon Mixing Method

Prep Time: 30 minutes

Cook Time: 25 minutes for layers and cupcakes/45 minutes for a sheet cake or tube pan

Total Time: 55 minutes for layers and cupcakes/1 hour 15 minutes for a sheet cake or tube pan

Dry Ingredients:

- 288 grams (2½ cups) cake flour
- 1 teaspoon baking powder
- ¼ teaspoon baking soda
- 300 grams (1½ cups) granulated sugar
- 3 grams (¾ teaspoon) fine sea salt

Wet Ingredients:

- 70 grams (5 tablespoons) unsalted butter, melted and cooled slightly

Continued on next page

This is my all-time favorite cake base recipe. I use this cake for most of my layer cakes. The flavor is incredibly rich and buttery while the cake is still super light and fluffy. Chiffon cake is traditionally baked in a tube pan, but this can also be baked into cake layers, a sheet cake, or cupcakes.

Method

Prep:

1. At least 30 minutes before preparing your batter, take the eggs and buttermilk out of the refrigerator to come to room temperature. Separate the eggs. Measure out the rest of the ingredients, keeping them in their groupings as laid out in the ingredient section.

2. Position an oven rack to the center position. Preheat the oven to 350°F/175°C.

3. If using a tube pan, grease only the bottom and not the sides of the tube. Alternatively, prepare your baking pan(s) with non-stick spray and parchment paper, or with paper liners if making cupcakes.

To Make the Cake:

1. Sift dry ingredients into a large bowl and then whisk together to combine. Set aside.

2. Whisk the wet ingredients together in a separate medium bowl and set aside.

3. In the bowl of a stand mixer fitted with the whisk attachment, or with a hand mixer, beat the egg whites on medium speed until they start forming soft peaks.

4. With the mixer still running, very slowly stream in the sugar and keep beating until you reach stiff peaks.

5. Pour the wet ingredients into the dry ingredient bowl and stir together with a rubber spatula just until the dry ingredients are saturated.

- 113 grams (½ cup, 120 milliliters) neutral oil (canola, vegetable, or avocado)
- 240 grams (1 cup, 240 milliliters) buttermilk, room temperature
- 2 teaspoons vanilla extract
- 105 grams (about 6 large) egg yolks, room temperature

Egg Foam:
- 95 grams (about 3 large) egg whites, room temperature
- 50 grams (¼ cup) granulated sugar

6. Start by adding about a quarter of the egg whites into the batter and stir it in completely to lighten the batter. Next add in half of the rest of the egg whites and gently fold them in, being careful not to deflate. Add in the rest of the egg whites and fold gently until completely combined.

7. Transfer the batter into your prepared pan(s). If making cupcakes, leave about ½ inch from the tops.

8. Bake at 350°F/175°C until a cake tester comes out clean. For cupcakes and layers, this should take about 20–25 minutes; for a tube cake or sheet cake, this should take about 40–45 minutes.

9. Set the cake(s) in the pan on a cooling rack until completely cooled before turning out.

10. Store uneaten cake covered at room temperature for up to 3 days.

Flavor Variation Ideas

♦ **Lemon Rosemary Cake:** *(this flavor may sound a bit different, but it is one of my favorite cakes of all time)* Add 1 tablespoon minced fresh rosemary into the dry ingredients and 1 tablespoon lemon zest into the wet ingredients. Pair with lemon cream cheese frosting (page 177).

♦ **Boston Cream Pie:** Make ½ batch of vanilla pastry cream (page 207) and allow it to cool completely. Meanwhile, bake the chiffon cake in two 9-inch (23-cm) layers and allow to cool completely. Spread the pastry cream between the two layers of cake. Make the small batch 1:1 ganache (page 253). Pour the ganache on top of the stacked layers, right in the center, allowing it to drip down the sides. Refrigerate for at least 2 hours before slicing.

Frostings

Knowing how to make a simple buttercream will open up a world of frosting flavors. It can be flavored in so many ways and paired with any cake variety. The most basic style of buttercream is called "American buttercream," which involves simply creaming butter and powdered sugar together. However, if you are interested in a more elevated style of buttercream, you can also make a "meringue buttercream," which involves whipping butter into meringue. This is covered in Chapter 8 when I show you how to make Swiss meringue (page 217).

 Frosting Tip! The key to making any frosting that isn't overly sweet is by making sure you include enough salt. If your frosting is tasting a bit too sweet, add another pinch of salt.

How to Fill a Piping Bag

If you want to pipe pretty swirls for your cupcakes or make any kind of designs on a layer cake, a piping bag is needed. If you will be using a piping tip with your bag, I highly recommend using a coupler. A coupler is a two-part plastic piece that goes in your bag and attaches the piping tip to the outside. This allows you to swap out your piping tips without switching bags.

To fill the bag, fit it with the coupler and piping tip, or cut the tip off if you aren't using a piping tip.

1. Place the bag in a tall cup and fold the top of the bag down. This will help the bag stay open while you add the frosting.

2. Then spoon your frosting into the bag, filling no more than two-thirds full.

3. Gently push the frosting down to the tip, making sure no air bubbles are trapped. Twist the end of the bag to keep closed.

VANILLA BUTTERCREAM FROSTING RECIPE

Yield: About 6 cups—enough for 24 cupcakes, a 3-layer 8-inch (20-cm) cake, or a 2-layer 9-inch (23-cm) cake (cut recipe in half for a 9 x 13-inch/23 x 33-cm sheet cake)

Specialty Equipment:
Hand mixer or stand mixer

Prep Time: 10 minutes

Total Time: 10 minutes

- 454 grams (2 cups, 4 sticks) unsalted butter, room temperature
- 600 grams (5 cups) powdered, icing, or confectioner's sugar
- 2 teaspoons vanilla extract
- 2 grams (½ teaspoon) kosher salt
- 56–84 grams (4–6 tablespoons) milk or heavy cream

This is the easiest style of buttercream to make and requires simply creaming together butter with powdered sugar and adding in any flavor you like! Use this as your base to make endless flavors to pair with your cakes.

Method

Prep:

1. At least 30 minutes before making the buttercream, take the butter out of the refrigerator to soften at room temperature.
2. Measure out the rest of the ingredients.

To Make the Buttercream:

1. In the bowl of a stand mixer fitted with a paddle attachment, or in a large mixing bowl with a hand mixer, beat the butter on medium speed for about 1 minute, until fluffy. Scrape down the sides and bottom of the bowl.
2. Add the powdered sugar into the mixing bowl and start mixing on low until the sugar starts to combine with the butter. Turn the mixing speed up to medium-high and beat for about 3 minutes until the mixture is light and fluffy. Mix in the vanilla extract and salt.
3. Add a bit of milk or heavy cream if needed to thin out the texture. If the texture becomes too thin, you can add a bit more powdered sugar until you get a spreadable consistency.
4. If not using immediately, store the buttercream in an airtight container in the refrigerator for up to 1 week. Allow to come back to room temperature and re-whip to use.

Flavor Variation Ideas

- ♦ **Chocolate Buttercream:** Add 107 grams (1⅓ cups) natural or Dutch-processed cocoa powder in with the powdered sugar. Add enough milk or cream to thin out the texture.

- ♦ **Coconut Buttercream:** Add in 1 teaspoon of coconut extract.

- ♦ **Citrus Buttercream (Lemon, Orange, or Lime):** Add in 3 tablespoons of citrus zest and 2 tablespoons of citrus juice. You likely will not need the milk to thin out.

- ♦ **Peanut Butter Buttercream:** Replace 227 grams (1 cup, 2 sticks) of butter with 254 grams (1 cup) of creamy peanut butter (or any other nut or seed butter). Reduce the powdered sugar to 420 grams (3 ½ cups).

- ♦ **Berry Buttercream (Strawberry, Raspberry, or Cherry):** Add 210 grams (¾ cup) seedless raspberry, strawberry, or cherry preserves in with the powdered sugar. You can also add a few drops of red food coloring if you like.

CREAM CHEESE FROSTING RECIPE

Yield: About 3 cups—enough for 12 cupcakes, two 8.5 x 4.5-inch (22 x 11-cm) loaf cakes, a 9 x 13-inch/23 x 33-cm sheet cake, or 1 batch of Cinnamon Rolls

Specialty Equipment:
Hand mixer or stand mixer

Prep Time: 10 minutes

Total Time: 10 minutes

- 226 grams (8 ounces) full-fat cream cheese, room temperature
- 57 grams (4 tablespoons, ½ stick) unsalted butter, room temperature
- 420 grams (3½ cups) powdered, icing, or confectioner's sugar
- 1 teaspoon vanilla
- ¼ teaspoon kosher salt

Cream cheese frosting is my favorite style of frosting. It's less sweet than buttercream and the tanginess really contrasts well with sweet cakes, and especially with cinnamon rolls (page 247)!

Method

Prep:

1. At least 1½ hours before making the frosting, take the cream cheese and butter out of the refrigerator to soften at room temperature. (I find cream cheese takes a very long time to come to room temp.)
2. Measure out the rest of the ingredients.

To Make the Frosting:

1. Place the cream cheese and butter in the bowl of a stand mixer fitted with a paddle attachment, or in a large mixing bowl with a hand mixer. Mix on medium speed for about 1 minute. Scrape down the sides.
2. Add the powdered sugar, vanilla, and salt into the mixing bowl and start mixing on low until the sugar starts to combine with the cream cheese mixture. Turn the mixing speed up to medium-high and beat for about 3 minutes, until the mixture is light and fluffy.
3. If not using immediately, store in an airtight container in the refrigerator for up to 1 week. Bring to room temperature and mix again before using.

Flavor Variation Ideas

- **Coconut Cream Cheese Frosting:** Add in ¾ teaspoon coconut extract.
- **Lemon, Orange, or Lime:** Add in 2 tablespoons of citrus zest with the powdered sugar.
- **Maple Cream Cheese Frosting:** Add in 1 teaspoon maple extract.

Layer Cakes

Building a simple layer cake is a formula consisting of three components: a cake layer, a frosting, and a filling. You can take any of the master cake recipes and frostings in this book to create a layer cake. For fillings, you can simply use the frosting that you choose to ice with as your filling. You could also use jams, curds (page 178), whipped cream (page 263), fresh fruit, ganache (page 253), or pastry cream (page 207).

Layers vs. Tiers

The layers of a cake are the individual cakes that are stacked and frosted together to make one taller singular cake. Cake tiers are when multiple layer cakes are stacked on top of each other to make a large cake display, like a wedding cake.

How to Stack a Simple Layer Cake

Bake the layers and let them cool completely. I like to make my layer cakes with three 8-inch (20-cm) layers, as I think the ratio looks best. It is also easier to frost cold cake, so I will often pop the layers in the freezer for 10–15 minutes before frosting.

1. Level the cake layers. Hold a serrated knife horizontally, resting it on the edge of the cake layer, and saw back and forth to cut off the dome of each layer.

2. Secure the first layer to the cake stand or cake board with a dollop of frosting.

3. Spread an even layer of frosting on top of the first layer. Alternatively, if using a filling, pipe a dam of frosting around the edge of the first layer and add the filling.

4. Place your second layer on top of the filling, upside down. This will help keep the cake very level and even. Gently press down to secure.

5. If this is a three-layer cake, add another layer of frosting or pipe another dam and add filling to the second layer.

6. Add the final layer, again upside down, and gently press to secure. Get down to eye level with your cake and make adjustments to make sure all layers are centered.

7. Add a generous amount of frosting to the top and sides of the cake. Use an offset spatula to spread it around to cover the cake.

8. Use an offset spatula to make sweeping motions for a classic wavy frosting look.

Chocolate Cream Pie (page 221)

8

Pies

There is a wide range of baked goods that fall into the pie category, including traditional pies, tarts, cobblers, crumbles, and crisps. You will be excited to know that, with a few base recipes in your arsenal, you can put together any one of these with ease.

Because this chapter covers a vast array of possible pie options, it is laid out a bit differently than the previous chapters. Following you will find recipes for various bases, fillings, and toppings, along with guidelines about how you can mix and match these components to build your desired pastry. The chapter ends with a chart of popular pies and how to use the components to build them.

Categories of Pie

All of the pies we are covering in this book consist of various combinations of a crust, a filling, and a topping. The ways in which these are combined and shaped determine which type has been created.

Traditional Pie

- **Base Options:** Traditional pie pastry, cookie crumb crust
- **Filling Options:** Fruit filling, cooked custards, pastry cream, savory meat and/or vegetable filling, no-bake fillings
- **Topping Options:** No topping, traditional pie pastry, streusel, meringue, whipped cream

A traditional pie typically consists of a classic pie pastry base and either a sweet or savory filling. Sweet pies often also use a cookie crumb crust (such as a graham cracker crust).

Traditional pies have the most combinations to choose from when making your creation. Start with a traditional pie crust, add an apple filling, and top with streusel, and you have a Dutch apple pie. Or start with a cookie crust, add a chocolate pastry cream filling and a whipped cream topping, and you have made a chocolate cream pie. The possibilities are truly endless.

Tart

- **Base Options:** Shortbread crust
- **Filling Options:** Curd, pastry cream, ganache
- **Topping Options:** No topping, fresh fruit, whipped cream, meringue

A tart is made in a shallower pan than a pie and has a thicker crust. Typically, a sweeter and more stable crust than traditional pie pastry is used—something like a shortbread crust. The filling also often sits more on top of the crust, rather than within the crust.

Berry Crisp (page 221)

Cobbler

- **Base Options:** N/A
- **Filling Options:** Fruit filling
- **Topping Options**: Biscuit topping

There are varying regional opinions about what a cobbler truly is. The most widely accepted definition is a fruit filling that is topped with a biscuit or dumpling type topping with no base crust. The biscuit dough is dropped over the fruit topping, which gives it the look of a cobbled road.

Crumbles & Crisps

- **Base Options:** N/A
- **Filling Options:** Fruit filling
- **Topping Options:** Classic streusel, oat or nut streusel

Crumbles and crisps are very similar in style to a cobbler, the only difference being the topping. A traditional streusel topping is used for a crumble, while an oat streusel or nut streusel topping is used for a crisp. These streusel toppings are sprinkled over a fruit filling, and just like with a cobbler, there is no base crust.

Pie Components

Now that we've established definitions for all of the different types of pies we are covering, I want to review the components used to create them. Some of these components are incredibly easy to put together. However, some require a bit more of an in-depth tutorial for proper technique.

Crusts

There are three types of crust options in this section: traditional pie pastry, cookie crumb crust, and shortbread crust. These options are going to be the most versatile in making the widest variety of pies.

Traditional Pie Pastry

Traditional pie pastry is extremely simple in its ingredients. The recipe calls for only flour, solid fat (butter, shortening, or lard), salt, and ice water. You can also choose to add a bit of sugar if you want a touch of sweetness in your crust. However, I prefer the contrast of a savory crust with a sweet filling.

The most important thing to keep in mind when making a pie pastry is controlling gluten development. In order to keep the crust flaky and tender, it's important to work the dough as little as possible once the water is added.

The method used for making a pie dough is actually very similar to the Biscuit Mixing Method we covered in Chapter 5. The solid fat is cut or rubbed into the dough and kept in solid pieces. These solid pieces will melt in the oven, creating little pockets of steam and flakiness.

If you read any number of pie crust tutorials, you will find a lot of different methods for how to work the fat into your flour. Some use a pastry blender, some use a food processor, while others use a mixer. You are welcome to experiment with these alternate methods to see if you prefer one over the other. However, I personally find that working the fat in with your fingers is not only the easiest method, but also very effective for getting a flaky crust.

Many people prefer an all-butter pie crust due to the flavor. I, however, prefer using mostly butter with a bit of shortening in my crust. The shortening will help the crust hold its shape and not shrink as much in the oven. It is also important that the water you use in your pie crust is really ice-cold. This will ensure that the fat stays solid as you are working your dough.

TRADITIONAL PIE PASTRY

Yield: Pastry for a single or double 9-inch (23-cm) deep dish pie
Specialty Equipment: Rolling pin
Prep Time: 1 hour 20 minutes

For a Single Crust

- 180 grams (1 ½ cups) all-purpose flour
- 2 grams (½ teaspoon) kosher salt
- 13 grams (1 tablespoon) granulated sugar, *optional*
- 85 grams (6 tablespoons) unsalted butter, cold
- 30 grams (2½ tablespoons) shortening
- 57–85 grams (4–6 tablespoons, 60–90 milliliters) ice water

For a Double Crust

- 360 grams (3 cups) all-purpose flour
- 5 grams (1 teaspoon) kosher salt
- 26 grams (2½ tablespoons) granulated sugar, *optional*
- 170 grams (12 tablespoons, 1 ½ sticks) unsalted butter, cold
- 60 grams (5 tablespoons) shortening
- 114–168 grams (8–12 tablespoons, 120–180 milliliters) ice water

This pie crust can be made as a single crust or as a double crust. The high ratio of butter in the crust makes it taste amazing, while the small addition of shortening helps it hold its shape better. My recipe for pie crust is a bit larger than most because I find that this helps avoid any frustration in making the dough large enough to fit the pie plate, especially for beginners.

Method

Prep:

1. Measure out all of the ingredients.
2. Cut the butter into small pieces, about ½ inch (1 cm) in size. Make sure it is very cold. If it has started to warm up, you can place it in the freezer for a few minutes before starting.

To Make the Dough:

1. In a large mixing bowl, whisk together the flour, salt, and sugar if using.
2. Add the shortening and cold butter to the bowl and toss with your hands so all of the fat is coated with flour. Use the tips of your fingers and thumbs to press down on all of the pieces of fat, creating little sheets of fat throughout your mixture. If it feels like the fat is starting to melt, pop the bowl in the refrigerator for 5–10 minutes before continuing. Continue working the fat through the flour until all of the fat has been worked through and it ranges in size from pea to walnut throughout.
3. Add the ice water little by little into the mixture. Fold the mixture gently with a silicone spatula to incorporate. Use a light hand to slowly hydrate the flour as you add more water. You may not need all of the water. Once large clumps of dough start forming, gather the dough up and press it together. If it crumbles, then you need to add a little more water. If it holds together, then you are ready to chill the dough.

4. Bring the dough together on your counter, press it into one mass, and knead very gently for one or two turns to bring it into a cohesive dough. If you made a double batch of dough, divide it in half.

5. Press flat into a round disk and wrap in plastic wrap. Chill in the refrigerator for a minimum of 30 minutes, but preferably an hour, to allow the gluten to relax and the flour to fully hydrate.

6. Lightly flour a clean work surface and place your chilled dough on top. Lightly flour the top of the dough and your rolling pin. As you roll the dough, lift it up, turn it, and redistribute flour underneath it every few rolls to prevent sticking. Roll the dough out to about 1 ½ to 2 inches (4–5 cm) wider than your pie dish all the way around. This is important so that your dough doesn't need to stretch to fit down into the plate, which can cause it to shrink.

7. Set the rolling pin in the middle and fold the dough in half over the rolling pin. Gently transfer it into the pie plate, unrolling it off the rolling pin.

8. Lift up on the sides of the crust to allow it to fall naturally into the pie plate without having to stretch it.

9. If there are places that don't have quite enough dough to hang over the edge, you can patch them with pieces from the other side.

10. If your pie will not have a pastry crust on top, trim the excess dough, leaving about a ½-inch overhang all the way around the pie plate. Fold the extra dough under, creating a lip all the way around. If you will have a top crust, you can leave the edges as is for now. (See page 214 for instruction on how to form a top crust.)

 Baking Science Note: A popular technique for making pie crust is to freeze the butter and shred it on a cheese grater rather than cutting it into the flour. I personally do not prefer this method because it does not allow the flour to get fully coated with the fat before adding the water, which makes controlling the gluten development more difficult.

Tips for Rolling Crust

- Focus your pressure across the dough instead of down into the table. This will help prevent sticking.
- If the crust is cracking while rolling, it may be too cold. Allow it to sit at room temperature for a few minutes before continuing. You can also use the warmth of your hands to press it back together.

How to Crimp

1. Start by folding the edge under all the way around the crust to create a lip.

2. To do a classic crimp, push your pointer finger into the lip on one side of the crust, while pushing your pointer finger and thumb in on the other side of the crust to create a scalloped look. Continue doing this all the way around the crust.

3. Alternatively, you can press the tines of a fork, or the rounded tip of a spoon, into the crust all the way around to create a different decorative look.

Baker Bettie's Better Baking Book

Blind Baking

Blind baking is the term for baking a pie crust, either partially or fully, without any filling in it. This is done for pies where the filling doesn't need to be baked, like cream pies. It is also often done for custard pies (like pumpkin pie) so that you can ensure the crust is fully cooked through by the time the filling is finished baking.

To Blind-Bake Your Crust:

1. Fit the crust to the pie plate and crimp the edges. Dock the crust a few times on the bottom and up the sides.
2. Place a piece of parchment paper on top of the pie crust and fill it with dry beans, rice, or pie weights; they should fill the pan all the way to the top. This will help the crust hold its shape and not shrink while baking. I typically use dried beans for this and save them to reuse.
3. I suggest placing your crust in the freezer for at least 10 minutes, or in the refrigerator for at least 30 minutes, to firm up before baking to prevent shrinkage.
4. Bake in the bottom third of the oven at 400°F/205°C for 20 minutes.
5. Remove the parchment paper and pie weights from the crust. Return the crust to the oven. **For a partially baked crust** (if the filling will also be baked), bake for another 6–8 minutes, until the bottom is just starting to set. **For a fully baked crust**, bake for another 12–15 minutes, until the bottom is golden brown and fully set.
6. If your filling will not be baked, let the crust cool completely before adding it. If your filling will be baked in the crust, you can add it as soon as it is ready.

COOKIE CRUMB CRUST RECIPE

Yield: Crust for one 9-inch (23-cm) deep dish pie

Specialty Equipment: Food processor (optional)

Prep Time: 10 minutes

Cook Time (optional): 8 minutes

Total Time: 10 minutes/18 minutes

- 200 grams (7 ounces, about 2 cups once made into crumbs) crisp cookie of choice (graham crackers, digestive biscuits, vanilla wafers, chocolate sandwich cookies, gingersnaps, etc.)
- 50 grams (¼ cup) granulated sugar
- 113 grams (½ cup, 1 stick) unsalted butter, melted

A cookie crumb crust is a very simple pie crust that is made up of three ingredients: premade cookies that have been crumbled, sugar, and melted butter. Essentially any cookie that has a crisp and crumbly texture can be utilized to make this type of crust. This includes graham crackers, gingersnaps, digestive biscuits, vanilla wafers, chocolate sandwich cookies, etc.

This type of crust can be used for any type of pie you would like, but it is most commonly used with cheesecakes, cream pies, and other no-bake pies.

Method

1. Place the cookies in a food processor and pulse until you have cookie crumbs. Alternatively, you can place them in a zip-top bag and use a rolling pin to roll back and forth over the cookies until they are crumbs. Pour the crumbs into a medium bowl.

2. Stir in the granulated sugar and the melted butter until all of the crumbs are completely coated with butter.

3. Firmly press the cookie crumb mixture into the bottom and up the sides of your pie plate or baking dish. The bottom of a glass or a measuring cup can be helpful to press the crumbs into an even layer.

4. This crust can be used baked or unbaked. A baked crust will have a crunchier texture and a slightly toasted flavor. If desired, bake at 375°F/190°C for 8 minutes. Allow to cool completely before filling the crust. If you are keeping the crust unbaked, place it in the refrigerator for about 10 minutes to firm up before filling.

Shortbread Crust

A shortbread crust is made from the same shortbread dough we used to make cookies. It creates a crust that is buttery, soft, and slightly sweeter than a traditional pie pastry. This style of crust is most traditionally used as the base for tarts, but it can be used for other types of pies as well, especially cheesecakes.

To make the crust, utilize the shortbread cookie recipe (page 136) and follow the instructions for using it as a base for a tart or pie.

Fillings

The variety of fillings that can be used for pies and pastries is vast. However, there are three main categories that cover the bulk of pie options: fruit filling, cooked custard filling, and cream pie/no-bake fillings.

Fruit Filling

Fruit pies are my favorite types of pies to make because they feel so comforting and nostalgic. Bringing a homemade apple pie to a gathering is sure to impress. I also love mixing different fruits together. Instead of making a pie with only apples, I often add raspberries in the summer or cranberries in the winter. The contrast really pops and makes the pie extra special.

Pies that are made with a fruit filling most often start with a traditional pie pastry as the base. The fruit filling can then be made with either fresh or frozen fruit, and the topping is usually additional pie pastry. Fruit pies can also be topped with streusel topping, such as with a Dutch apple pie.

Preventing a Soggy Bottom

One of the most common issues with fruit-filled pies is a soggy bottom or a filling that is runny. Some methods call for the fruit or its juices to be precooked, before adding it to the crust, to prevent this. However, you can definitely make an uncooked fruit-filled pie that isn't soggy or runny.

Fruits release a lot of juice when baked, and it is important that it thickens fully before the baked good is removed from the oven. Oftentimes a fruit pie is runny simply because it didn't bake long enough. Here are a few tips for preventing a soggy bottom with fruit-filled pies:

- Bake the pie in the bottom third of the oven on a preheated sheet pan or baking stone. The hot surface will help set the crust quickly.
- Mix the filling right before adding it to the crust. Mixing it too early will draw out too many juices, which will make the crust soggy before it sets.
- Make sure that the filling is rapidly bubbling in the center of the pie, not just on the edges, before removing it from the oven.
- Allow the pie to cool completely before slicing it. This will allow the filling to fully thicken.

Best Apples for Apple Pie

Not all apples are ideal baking apples. The best apples for baking are those that stand up well to heat and do not break down too much as they are baked.

Granny Smith apples are known as baking apples, and I love their tart quality mixed with sugar in a filling. I do, however, prefer to combine them with other sweeter apples. Golden Delicious and Honeycrisp are two of my favorite varieties to mix with Granny Smiths.

Classic Apple Pie. Components: Traditional Pie Pastry (page 187), Fruit Filling (page 197)

FRUIT PIE FILLING MASTER RECIPE

Yield: Filling for a 9-inch (23-cm) deep dish pie, or for a 9 x 13-inch (23 x 33-cm) crisp, crumble, or cobbler
Prep Time: 20 minutes

- 900 grams (2 pounds) fresh or frozen fruit (this is the weight of the fruit actually going in the pie. Make sure to account for extra weight when purchasing fruit, like apples, where the core will be discarded)
- 100 grams-150 grams (½ cup to ¾ cup) granulated sugar or brown sugar (use less sugar for very sweet fruits like apples and cherries, and more sugar for very tart fruits like rhubarb and raspberries)
- 30 grams (¼ cup) cornstarch
- 1 gram (¼ teaspoon) kosher salt
- 30 grams (2 tablespoons) acidic liquid (lemon juice, orange juice, lime juice, apple cider vinegar)
- 28 grams (2 tablespoons) butter, cut into small pieces

This is my basic formula for creating a fruit pie filling as well as for crisps, crumbles, and cobblers. Fresh or frozen fruit can be used here, but keep in mind that frozen fruit does release more liquid and will need a bit longer in the oven.

Method

To Make the Fruit Filling:

1. If using frozen fruit, thaw completely and drain the excess juices off so that the filling is not too soupy.

2. Prepare the crust and topping for your recipe before preparing the fruit filling. Combining the fruit with the sugar too early will release too much juice.

3. Prepare your chosen fruit by peeling, coring, pitting, and/or slicing if necessary. Apples and pears should be sliced to about ¼ inch thick; strawberries can be quartered. Things like blueberries, cherries, cranberries, and raspberries can be left whole.

4. Combine the fruit, sugar, cornstarch, salt, and your acidic ingredient together. Add any extracts, zests, or spices if using. Gently stir with a spoon or spatula until everything is evenly incorporated.

5. The butter will be dotted on top of the filling before adding the topping.

Flavoring Your Fruit Filling

You can add spices and/or zest to your filling to give it even more flavor.

Spices

(Use up to 2 teaspoons total of combined spices if desired)

- 1–2 teaspoons cinnamon
- ½ teaspoon ginger
- ¼ teaspoon nutmeg
- ¼ teaspoon cardamom
- ⅛ teaspoon clove
- ⅛ teaspoon allspice

Extracts & Zests

(Use 1–2 if desired)

- 1½ teaspoons vanilla extract
- ½ teaspoon almond extract
- ¼ teaspoon anise extract
- 2 tablespoons lemon, orange, or lime zest

Traditional Fruit Pie

Yield: One 9-inch (23-cm) deep dish pie

Prep + Chilling Time: 1 hour

Cook Time: 1 hour 5 minutes

Total Time: 2 hours 5 minutes

1. Prepare a double-crust pie pastry (page 187) at least 30 minutes before baking your pie, and place in the refrigerator to chill.

2. Position an oven rack in the bottom third of the oven and place a sheet pan or baking stone on it to preheat. The pie will bake on the preheated surface, which will prevent a soggy crust.

3. Preheat the oven to 400°F/205°C.

4. Roll out half of the pie dough and fit a 9-inch (23-cm) pie plate with it. Do not crimp the edges. Place in the refrigerator while you prepare your filling.

5. Prepare the fruit filling. Add the filling to your pie plate with your raw bottom crust. Dot the butter all around the top of the filling.

6. Roll out your top crust and fit it over the top of your filling (see page 189 for demo).

7. Trim the edges and crimp.

8. Brush the top with egg wash (page 255) and sprinkle with sugar if desired.

9. Place the pie on a sheet pan lined with foil (to catch any spillage) and place it on the preheated surface. Bake at 400°F/205°C for 30 minutes, then turn down the heat to 350°F/175°C and bake for an additional 20–35 minutes until the filling is rapidly bubbling in the center, not just on the edges. Watch the crust and lay a piece of foil over the top of the pie once it is finished browning, usually around the 45-minute mark.

10. Remove from the oven to a cooling rack and let cool for a minimum of 3 hours before slicing to allow the filling to thicken.

11. Fruit pies can be stored covered in the refrigerator for up to 3 days.

Fruit Cobbler

Yield: One 9 x 13-inch (23 x 33-cm) cobbler

Prep Time: 30 minutes

Cook Time: 1 Hour

Total Time: 1 Hour 30 Minutes

1. Position an oven rack to the center position and preheat the oven to 350°F/175°C.
2. Grease a 9 x 13-inch (23 x 33-cm) baking dish with butter or non-stick spray.
3. Prepare the fruit filling and add it to your baking dish. Dot the butter all around the top of the filling.
4. Follow the recipe for the buttermilk biscuit dough (page 107) through step 4, using the sugar in the recipe.
5. Break off pieces of the dough, flatten them out slightly, and top the fruit with it. The topping will spread out as it bakes, so it is okay if there are gaps.
6. Brush the topping with melted butter and sprinkle with sugar if desired.
7. Bake at 350°F/175°C for 50–60 minutes, until the biscuits are cooked through and the filling is bubbling.
8. Allow to cool for at least 15 minutes before serving.
9. Store leftover cobbler covered in the refrigerator for up to 3 days.

Fruit Crisp or Crumble

Yield: One 9 x 13-inch (23 x 33-cm) cobbler

Prep Time: 30 minutes

Cook Time: 50 minutes

Total Time: 1 hour 20 minutes

1. Position an oven rack to the center position and preheat the oven to 350°F/175°C.
2. Grease a 9 x 13-inch (23 x 33-cm) baking dish with butter or non-stick spray.
3. Prepare the fruit filling and add it to your baking dish. Dot the butter all around the top of the filling.
4. Prepare a double batch of streusel topping (page 261, any variation you like) and sprinkle it evenly over the top of the filling.
5. Bake at 350°F/175°C for 45–50 minutes, until the filling is bubbly. If the topping is getting too brown, you can tent a piece of foil over the dish during the last part of baking.
6. Store leftover crisp or crumble covered in the refrigerator for up to 3 days.

Baked Custard Filling

Baked custard pie fillings include pumpkin pie, pecan pie, cheesecake, chess pie, and many others. These types of fillings are made with eggs and are fairly liquid before baking. The filling is then baked in the crust, rather than being cooked separately and combined as with cream pies.

Custard pies are typically made with traditional pie pastry or cookie crumb crusts. Custard pies also typically don't have a topping as part of the pie. Rather, whipped cream is typically offered on the side as an optional accompaniment. Because there is such a wide variety of custard fillings, most varieties are fairly individual, and I don't typically work from master recipes (that is, with the exception of cheesecake). As a general rule of thumb, it is typically recommended to blind-bake the crust partially before adding your custard filling to finish baking the pie. This will ensure that the bottom of your crust is fully cooked through and will not become soggy.

Preventing Cracking with Cooked Custard Fillings

Cooked custard pies are notorious for cracking. This issue can stem from several different sources, including mixing technique, baking temperature, and the cooling process.

When mixing a cooked custard filling, take extra care not to beat air into it. Too much air in the filling will cause it to inflate in the oven and then collapse, which causes cracking. This means it is also extra important that all of your ingredients are truly at room temperature before mixing, so that they will easily blend together to make smooth filling.

Baking a custard at a high temperature can also cause it to crack for a similar reason. The liquid will quickly evaporate off, causing the filling to rise and then fall. For this reason, many recipes call either for the pie to be baked at a low temperature for a very long time, or for a water bath to be used. A water bath consists of a larger pan that is filled with hot water and the pie or cheesecake is set into it, so that hot water surrounds the outside of the baking dish. This helps to keep a lower, even temperature around the pie and helps keep it moist to help prevent cracking.

The last point at which a custard pie can crack is if it cools too quickly. Many cheesecake recipes may call for it to be left in an oven that is turned off for an extended period of time after baking to help it slowly cool. You also want to make sure you do not move your custard pie or cheesecake into the refrigerator until it has come completely to room temperature.

Even with all of this extra care, you might still get a crack in your pie. If you do, don't fret! You can easily hide the imperfections with fresh fruit topping, whipped cream, or baked cut-out pie crust pieces. It will still taste just as delicious!

Components: Chocolate Graham Cracker Crust (page 193), Vanilla Cheesecake Filling (page 203),
Caramel Sauce Drizzle (page 251), Ganache Drizzle (page 253)

Classic Cheesecake with Raspberry Sauce
Components: Cookie Crumb Crust (page 193), Berry Sauce (page 250)

CHEESECAKE MASTER RECIPE

Yield: 12 servings

Specialty Equipment: 9-inch (23-cm) spring form pan

Prep Time: 20 minutes

Cook Time: 1 hour 58 minutes

Total Time: 2 hours 18 minutes

- Prepared crust of choice; a cookie crumb crust (page 193) or a shortbread crust (page 136) is recommended
- 678 grams (three 8-oz. packages) full-fat cream cheese, room temperature
- 225 grams (1 cup + 2 tablespoons) granulated sugar
- 15 grams (2 tablespoons) all-purpose flour
- 3 large eggs, room temperature
- 180 grams (¾ cup) sour cream, room temperature
- ½ teaspoon vanilla extract
- ½ teaspoon lemon zest (*optional, but recommended if making a plain cheesecake, as it enhances the tangy flavor of a classic cheesecake)

This base recipe for cheesecake is incredibly creamy and delicious as is, and in fact, that is how I most often make it. However, this recipe can also be your starting point for making a wide variety of flavors.

With this cheesecake method, I do not call for using a water bath; rather, we start baking the cheesecake at a high temperature for a short amount of time to set the crust, and then a lower temperature for a long time to prevent it from cracking. This eliminates the need for a water bath.

Method

Prep:

1. 1½ hours before preparing the cheesecake, set out the cream cheese, eggs, and sour cream to come to room temperature. It is extremely important for a creamy cheesecake that your ingredients are not cold. (I find cream cheese takes a very long time to come to room temp.)
2. Prepare your crust of choice in a spring form pan.
3. Position an oven rack to the center position and preheat the oven to 450°F/230°C.

To Make the Filling:

1. In the bowl of a stand mixer fitted with a paddle attachment, or in a large bowl with a hand mixer, combine the cream cheese, sugar, and flour and beat on medium speed for 2 minutes, until well combined. You want it to be very smooth, but you don't want to whip too much air into it. Scrape down the bowl.
2. Add the eggs one at a time while the mixer is running on low speed. Scrape down the sides and bottom of the bowl.
3. Add the sour cream, vanilla, and any other extracts, spices, and zests if using. Mix on low speed until incorporated. Scrape down the sides and bottom of the bowl to ensure all of the mixture is evenly combined.
4. Pour the mixture into the prepared crust.

5. Bake at 450°F/230°C for 8 minutes. *Leave the door closed* and reduce the oven temperature to 200°F/93°C for 50 minutes. Turn the oven off (again, do not open the oven door!) and leave the cheesecake in the turned-off oven for 1 hour.

6. Remove the cheesecake from the oven and let sit until it is completely at room temperature (around 2 hours). Cover the cheesecake (still in the pan) with plastic wrap or foil and refrigerate for at least 6–8 hours before removing the sides of the pan and slicing.

7. Store leftover cheesecake covered in the refrigerator for up to 1 week. To store the cheesecake in the freezer, freeze it uncovered until solid, then wrap it well in plastic wrap and/or foil and store in the freezer for up to 3 months. To thaw, unwrap and place in the refrigerator overnight.

Flavoring Your Cheesecake

Here are a variety of options for creating different flavors of cheesecake utilizing the base recipe.

Spices

(Use up to 2 teaspoons total combined spices if desired)

- 1–2 teaspoons cinnamon
- ½ teaspoon ginger
- ¼ teaspoon nutmeg
- ¼ teaspoon cardamom
- ⅛ teaspoon clove

Topping Options

(Serve over the baked cheesecake if desired)

- fruit curd (page 211)
- chocolate ganache (page 253, 1:1 small batch)
- caramel sauce (page 251)
- berry sauce (page 250)

Extracts, Zests, & Juices

(Use 1–2 of these if desired)

- 1½ teaspoons vanilla extract
- ½ teaspoon almond extract
- ¼ teaspoon anise extract
- 2 tablespoons lemon, orange, or lime zest + 2 tablespoons lemon, orange, or lime juice

No-Bake & Cream Pie Fillings

No-bake pies are made with fillings that do not require baking in the oven. This includes cream pie filling, which is made from pastry cream (essentially homemade pudding), as well as chiffon pies and other chilled pie fillings.

These types of pies are typically made with either a traditional pastry crust or a graham cracker crust. If using a traditional pie pastry, you will want to blind-bake the crust fully because the pie will not be going back into the oven once the filling is added. Allow the crust to cool completely before adding your filling. If you are using a graham cracker crust, you can either leave it unbaked, or bake it and allow it to cool completely before adding your filling.

Lemon Meringue Pie (page 222) Components: Traditional Pie Pastry (187),
Lemon Curd (211), Swiss Meringue (217)

Chocolate Cream Pie (page 221)
Components: Cookie Crumb Crust (page 193), Pastry Cream (page 207), Whipped Cream (page 263)

PASTRY CREAM MASTER RECIPE

Yield: About 3 cups; enough to full a 9-inch (23-cm) deep dish pie

Specialty Equipment:

Fine mesh sieve

Prep Time: 10 minutes

Cook Time: 15 minutes

Total Time: 25 minutes

- 100 grams (½ cup) granulated sugar
- 110 grams (6 large) egg yolks
- 30 grams (¼ cup) cornstarch
- 1 gram (¼ teaspoon) kosher salt
- 568 grams (2½ cups, 600 milliliters) whole milk
- 1 ½ teaspoons vanilla extract or vanilla paste (optional)
- 28 grams (2 tablespoons) unsalted butter, cut into small pieces

My favorite use for pastry cream is as the filling for a cream pie. It can also be used in a wide variety of ways, including filling cakes and other pastries (such as eclairs). Basic pastry cream is traditionally flavored with vanilla and is incredibly delicious as is. Layer it in a pie crust with fresh sliced bananas and you have an incredible banana cream pie. Swap out the dairy milk for coconut milk and you have a creamy filling for coconut cream pie.

Method

Prep:

1. Measure out all of the ingredients. Cut the butter into small pieces.

To Make the Pastry Cream:

1. In a large mixing bowl use a whisk to beat the egg yolks with the sugar, cornstarch, and salt until foamy and about double in size. This will ensure a smooth pastry cream.

2. In a saucepan, heat the milk until it starts to boil.

3. Temper the egg yolks by slowly pouring about half of the milk into the egg/cornstarch mixture while whisking continuously. It can be helpful to nestle the mixing bowl in a damp kitchen towel to stabilize the bowl while you whisk and pour.

4. Pour the milk/egg mixture back into the pot with the remainder of the milk and cook over low heat, whisking continuously, until the mixture thickens and starts rapidly bubbling. Do not rush this process.

5. Pour the hot pastry cream through a fine mesh sieve.

6. If you are adding any chocolate or other flavorings, they can be whisked in at this point. Add the butter and vanilla and whisk in.

7. Place a piece of plastic wrap right on top of the pastry cream and refrigerate until ready to use.

8. Pastry cream can be stored in an airtight container in the refrigerator for up to 3 days.

Flavoring Pastry Cream

- **Chocolate Pastry Cream:** Add 10 grams (2 tablespoons) unsweetened cocoa powder in with the milk when you bring it to a boil. After the mixture has been strained, stir in 168 grams (6 ounces) of finely chopped bittersweet or semi-sweet chocolate.
- **Coconut Pastry Cream:** Replace 113 grams (½ cup) of the milk with 120 grams (½ cup) full-fat coconut milk. 100 grams (1 cup) of toasted coconut flakes can also be added to the filling before placing in the pie shell.

- **Peanut Butter Pastry Cream:** Whisk 127 grams (½ cup) creamy peanut butter into the mixture after it has gone through the sieve. Omit the butter.

Cream Pie

1. Prepare the pastry cream and place in the refrigerator to chill until ready to use.
2. Prepare a crust with either traditional pie pastry (page 187) or a cookie crumb crust (page 193). If using traditional pie pastry, blind-bake until fully cooked and allow to cool completely. If using a cookie crumb crust, you can either leave it unbaked or bake the crust and allow it to cool fully.
3. Pour the pastry cream into your prepared crust. The pastry cream does not need to be completely cool, but do not add it when it is extremely hot.
4. Place a piece of plastic wrap on top of the filling and refrigerate until completely cool (at least 2 hours).
5. Right before serving, top with whipped cream (page 263).

Pastry Cream Fruit Tart

1. Make the pastry cream and allow it to cool completely.
2. Meanwhile, make a shortbread tart crust (page 136) and bake it fully. Allow to cool completely.
3. Spread the pastry cream on top of your cooled tart crust and top with your fruit of choice.
4. Brush a fruit glaze (page 255) over the fruit.
5. Chill for at least 2 hours before serving.

To Use Pastry Cream as a Cake Filling

1. Make a half-batch of pastry cream and allow it to cool completely.
2. Spread between the cooled cake layers (detailed on page 179).

Banana Cream Pie (page 221)

Components: Traditional Pie Pastry (page 187), Vanilla Pastry Cream (page 207), Whipped Cream (page 263)

Blood Orange Curd Fruit Tart
Components: Shortbread Crust (page 136), Fruit Curd (page 211), Fruit Glaze (page 255)

FRUIT CURD MASTER RECIPE

Yield: About 3 cups

Specialty Equipment:

Fine mesh sieve

Prep Time: 5 minutes

Cook Time: 10 minutes

Total Time: 15 minutes

- 145 grams (8 large) egg yolks
- 38 grams (5 tablespoons) cornstarch, *optional* (use if you want a curd that will be firm and sliceable once chilled)
- 267 grams (1⅓ cups) granulated sugar
- 1 gram (¼ teaspoon) kosher salt
- 340 grams (1½ cups, 360 milliliters) unsweetened fruit juice (tart fruits work best: lemon, lime, orange, cranberry, grapefruit, or a combination)
- 2 teaspoons citrus zest, *optional*
- 85 grams (6 tablespoons) unsalted butter, cubed

Fruit curd is one of my favorite pastry components! Lemon curd is the most common type, but you can utilize any tart fruit juice to make a fruit curd. Lemon, lime, orange, cranberry, and grapefruit juice all work well. Make sure that, if you use bottled juice (for instance, cranberry juice), it's the kind that is unsweetened and 100 percent juice. I love a very tart curd, so I typically will use at least some lemon juice in any curd I make.

Fruit curds are used commonly as the filling of a pie or topping for a tart. They can also be used to fill a cake, or as a topping for scones. If you want a soft, spreadable curd, omit the cornstarch in the recipe. But if you want the curd to set firm and be sliceable, use the cornstarch to stabilize it.

Method

1. Whisk the egg yolks together in a medium bowl and set aside.
2. In a medium saucepan, whisk the cornstarch (if using), sugar, salt, and fruit juice together.
3. Heat over medium heat, whisking continuously, until the mixture comes to a boil and thickens.
4. Once the mixture has boiled for about 1 minute and has thickened, temper the egg yolks by slowly streaming in about a third of the hot liquid while whisking continuously.
5. Add the egg yolk mixture into the pot with the rest of the hot liquid and continue heating on medium heat while whisking continuously. When the mixture comes back to a boil, cook for about 3 minutes longer.
6. Pour the curd through a fine mesh sieve into a bowl. Add the zest (if using) and the butter and whisk to combine.
7. If not using immediately, place a piece of plastic wrap right on top of the curd to prevent a film from forming, and place in the refrigerator for up to 1 week.

 Note: Fruit curd tastes pretty eggy while it is warm. Once it cools down, this taste will subside.

To Use in a Meringue Pie

1. Blind-bake (page 191) a traditional pie pastry (page 187) until fully cooked through.
2. Make the curd and pour into the prepared crust. Place a piece of plastic wrap right on top of the curd to prevent a film from forming. Set aside to cool.
3. Make the meringue (page 217).
4. Add the meringue to the curd. If it hasn't cooled completely, that is okay, but do not add when the filling is very hot. Make sure you seal it all the way to the crust of the pie to prevent shrinking.
5. Place in the oven at 425°F/220°C for 4–5 minutes until the meringue is lightly toasted.
6. Allow to cool completely at room temperature, then refrigerate for at least 3 hours before serving. If you refrigerate while still warm, it may start weeping.

To Use in a Fruit Curd Tart

1. Make a shortbread tart crust (page 136) and blind-bake it fully.
2. Meanwhile, make the curd.
3. Pour the curd into the prepared tart crust and allow to cool at room temperature for 30 minutes, then refrigerate for at least 3 hours before serving.
4. If desired, top with fresh fruit and brush the fruit with glaze (page 255).
5. Dust with powdered sugar if desired.

To Use Curd as a Cake Filling

1. Make a half-batch of curd and allow to cool completely.
2. Spread between the cooled cake layers (detailed on page 179).

Toppings

The topping you chose to use for your pie relies heavily on what variety you are making. For instance, a biscuit topping is only used for cobblers, while a streusel topping can be used for several varieties, including fruit pies, crisps, and crumbles.

Double Pie Crust

Fruit pies are the main style of pie that is made with a top crust of traditional pie pastry. This is also used for savory pies, like chicken pot pie.

The pastry is made exactly the same way you make it for the bottom crust. In fact, the base recipe given previously makes enough dough for both a bottom and a top crust. I do suggest, however, that you roll your top crust out slightly thicker than you do your bottom crust, especially if you will make a lattice crust. This way the dough will be more stable and easier to work with.

Streusel Topping

Streusel (page 261) is a crumbly mixture of flour, butter, and sugar. It often also has nuts and/or oats added to it as well. This mixture can be placed on top of a pie in lieu of a traditional pastry crust. Streusel topping is most commonly used on a fruit pie, a crisp, or a crumble, and should be added right before the pie goes into the oven.

Make sure to keep an eye on the streusel topping. If it looks as though it is getting too browned, you can tent a piece of foil over it to prevent it from burning while the pie finishes cooking.

Whipped Cream Topping

Whipped cream (page 263) is the most common topping for cream pies. It is important that your pastry cream is completely cooled before you add your whipped cream on top, otherwise it will start to melt. I also suggest waiting to add the whipped cream until right before you serve your pie. Whipped cream is not very stable, and it will start to deflate after 24 hours.

Biscuit Topping

A biscuit topping (page 107) is used on cobblers. I recommend using the optional sugar in the biscuit recipe. Once you make up your dough, drop small portions of it evenly over your fruit filling, leaving room between them for some fruit to peek through. Before baking, brush the biscuit topping with some melted butter to help with browning. You can also sprinkle some sugar over the top, if you like, for additional texture.

Meringue Topping

Meringue, in its most basic form, is made from simply whipping raw egg whites with sugar until it becomes a fluffy and glossy mixture that holds stiff peaks. This style of meringue is called "French meringue," and it is what we made in Chapter 7 to make Angel Food Cake and Chiffon Cake.

While French meringue can be used as a topping for a pie or tart, it is the least stable style of meringue. It often weeps after a few hours, and I don't find the texture very appealing as a pie topping. It is well worth the effort to make Swiss meringue for the added benefits of its stability and superior texture.

How to Add a Top Crust to a Pie

To Make a Basic Top Crust:

1. Roll your dough out to about 1 inch (2.5 cm) wider than your pie dish all the way around and about ⅛ inch thick.
2. Transfer the rolled-out dough onto your filled pie plate. Cut a few slits in the center of the dough with a sharp knife to allow steam to escape while baking.
3. Trim the edges of your dough to about ½ inch wider than your pie plate. Fold the edge under all the way around, pressing to seal the top and bottom crust together.
4. Crimp as you would with a single crust.
5. Brush with an egg wash (page 255) and sprinkle with granulated sugar if desired.

To Make a Lattice Crust:

1. Roll your dough out to about 1 inch (2.5 cm) wider than your pie dish all the way around and about ⅛-inch thick.
2. Cut the dough into strips that are equal in width—about 1 inch (2.5 cm) each.
3. Take every other strip and lay them going one direction over your filled pie, spaced about 1 inch (2.5 cm) apart.
4. Fold every other strip halfway back, and lay a strip of dough down the center of the pie, going the opposite direction.
5. Unfold the pieces of dough back down over the new piece. Now fold back the other pieces that were not folded back the first time. Lay another piece of dough over the filling.
6. Repeat this process until you have the top covered with woven pieces of dough.
7. Trim the edges of your dough to about ½ inch wider than your pie plate. Fold the edge under all the way around, pressing to seal the top and bottom crust together.
8. Crimp as you would with a single crust.
9. Brush with an egg wash (page 255) and sprinkle with granulated sugar if desired.

Lemon Meringue Pie (page 222)
Components: Traditional Pie Pastry (page 187), Fruit Curd (page 217), Meringue Topping (page 217)

SWISS MERINGUE RECIPE

Yield: Enough to top a
9-inch (23-cm) pie or tart
Specialty Equipment:
Stand mixer or hand mixer
Prep Time: 10 minutes
Cook Time: 5 minutes
Total Time: 15 minutes

- 160 grams (about 5 large) egg whites, room temperature
- ½ teaspoon cream of tartar
- 225 grams (1 cup + 2 tablespoons) granulated sugar
- ¼ teaspoon kosher salt
- 1 teaspoon vanilla extract

Swiss meringue is a style of meringue that involves heating egg whites with sugar over a double boiler. Heating the mixture makes it more stable and makes a meringue that is silky-smooth in texture. Swiss meringue can also be made into a frosting called Swiss meringue buttercream. Many people prefer this style of buttercream to American buttercream because it is smoother and less sweet.

Method

Prep:
1. Set a medium saucepan, filled about halfway with water, on the stove over medium-low heat and bring to a simmer.
2. Separate the egg whites from the egg yolks. Measure out the rest of the ingredients.

To Make the Meringue:
1. Combine all of the ingredients together in the bowl of a stand mixer, or in a heatproof bowl. Whisk to combine.
2. Set the bowl over the pan of simmering water. If the water is touching the bowl, pour a bit of it out.
3. Stir with the whisk continuously, but do not whip air into the mixture. Check the mixture periodically by rubbing it between your fingers until there is no grittiness. If you have a thermometer, the mixture should reach 160°F/71°C.
4. Once the mixture feels smooth between your fingers, transfer the bowl to a stand mixer fitted with a whisk attachment. Alternatively, you can use a hand mixer.
5. Whip on medium-high speed until the mixture cools down and holds stiff peaks, about 5–7 minutes.
6. Use immediately.

How to Use Meringue on a Pie or Tart

1. Apply the meringue to the filling that has cooled slightly.
2. The easiest method of applying meringue is to use a rubber spatula and simply pile it on top. Make sure you "seal" the topping all the way to the edge of the pie so it touches the crust. This will help keep it from shrinking.
3. After your topping is added, you can leave it as is. It will harden slightly as it sits. Or bake at 425°F/220°C for 4–5 minutes, until lightly browned.
4. Allow the pie to cool completely before refrigerating, then chill for at least 3 hours before serving.

To Make Swiss Meringue Buttercream

1. Cut 454 grams (1 pound, 4 sticks) of unsalted butter into cubes and let sit at room temperature while you make the meringue. It doesn't need to be completely at room temperature.
2. Make the Swiss meringue.
3. Once the bowl is cool to the touch, add chunks of the butter into the meringue while the mixer is still running.
4. The meringue will start breaking down and look very curdled. This is normal!
5. Keep whipping after all the butter is added until the texture becomes smooth and fluffy.
6. Use to frost cake or cupcakes.

Peach Cobbler (page 222)
Components: Fruit Pie Filling (page 197), Biscuit Topping (page 107)

POPULAR PIE FLAVOR COMBINATIONS

Banana Cream Pie

1. Fully blind-bake a single-crust traditional pie pastry (page 187).
2. Make vanilla pastry cream (page 207) and allow it to cool fully.
3. Lay a single layer of sliced bananas in the cooled pie crust.
4. Add half of the pastry cream over the bananas and top with more sliced bananas.
5. Add the rest of the pastry cream.
6. Top with whipped cream (page 263).

Berry Crisp

1. Make the fruit pie filling (page 197) with a combination of berries such as blueberries, strawberries, raspberries, and cherries.
2. Put in a 9 x 13-inch (23 x 33-cm) dish.
3. Top with oat streusel topping (page 261).
4. Bake at 350°F/175°C for 50–60 minutes until the filling is bubbling.

Chocolate Cream Pie

1. Prepare chocolate pastry cream (page 208) and allow it to cool fully.
2. Make a chocolate cookie crumb crust (page 193).
3. Add the pastry cream into the prepared crust and top with whipped cream (page 263).
4. You can also add mini chocolate chips or chocolate shavings on top.

Coconut Cream Pie

1. Fully blind-bake a single-crust traditional pie pastry (page 187) and cool.
2. Make coconut pastry cream (page 208).
3. Add the pastry cream into the cooled crust and top with whipped cream (page 263) and toasted coconut flakes (page 256).

Dutch Apple Pie

1. Make a single traditional pastry crust (page 187) and do not blind-bake.
2. Add the fruit filling made with apples and 1 teaspoon cinnamon, ¼ teaspoon ginger, and ¼ teaspoon nutmeg.
3. Top with oat streusel topping (page 261).
4. Bake on a preheated sheet pan or baking stone at 400°F/205°C for 30 minutes, and then for an additional 20–35 minutes at 350°F/175°C.

Lemon Meringue Pie

1. Make a single traditional pastry crust (page 187) and fully blind-bake.
2. Make lemon curd with the cornstarch in the recipe (page 211) and set aside to cool slightly.
3. Add the curd to the prepared pie crust and cover with plastic wrap so a film doesn't form.
4. Make meringue topping (page 217).
5. Top curd with the meringue topping.
6. Bake at 425°F/220°C for 4–5 minutes until browned.

Peach Cobbler

1. Make the fruit pie filling (page 197) with peaches and brown sugar. Add ½ teaspoon cinnamon to the filling.
2. Put in a 9 x 13-inch (23 x 33-cm) dish.
3. Make the biscuit topping (page107) with the sugar in the recipe and dollop over the top of the fruit filling.
4. Brush the topping with melted butter.
5. Combine 25 grams (2 tablespoons) granulated sugar with ½ teaspoon sugar and pinch of clove. Sprinkle over the topping.
6. Bake at 350°F/175°C for 50–60 minutes.

Strawberry Rhubarb Pie

1. Make a double-crust pie pastry (page 187).
2. Make the fruit filling (page 197) with half strawberries and half rhubarb.
3. Fit the pie plate with pie pastry, add the filling, and top with the rest of the pie pastry. I recommend a lattice crust.
4. Bake on a preheated sheet pan or baking stone at 400°F/205°C for 30 minutes, and then for an additional 20–35 minutes at 350°F/175°C.

Strawberry Rhubarb Pie (page 222)

Soft Dinner Rolls (page 247)

9

Yeast Breads

Bread baking is my favorite subject to teach. It is so rewarding to take such simple ingredients and watch them transform into something so incredibly beautiful and delicious.

I have found that even experienced bakers can feel intimidated by making bread. My goal is to break it down here and make it very approachable for you. Bread can be one of the simplest things you can bake, and yet can also become very advanced and require many years of practice to master. We are starting on the simple end of that spectrum!

My goal for you is to finish this section with a clear understanding of how yeast works, and confidence in the basic process of making bread. I should also mention that you do not need any fancy equipment to bake bread. No stand mixer or bread machine needed! We are making it all by hand.

What is Yeast?

Yeast is a fungus, it is alive, and it happens to be everywhere. Baker's yeast is used to leaven and flavor breads and some pastries through the process of fermentation.

Dry Yeast for Baking

Dry yeast is a strain of yeast cultivated specifically for its ability to work very quickly and efficiently to make bread rise. The yeast cells have been dried out, and therefore are in a dormant state. Dry yeast is sold in two main forms: Active dry yeast and instant yeast (also known as quick-rise or rapid-rise yeast).

Active dry yeast and instant yeast function essentially the same way, with the main difference being the rate of activity. Active dry yeast contains larger yeast cells that work a little slower than the smaller instant yeast cells. Active dry and instant yeast can almost always be used interchangeably. Just be aware that your rising times will be longer with active dry yeast than with instant yeast.

How Yeast Functions

Yeast needs two main things to thrive: moisture and a food source. Sugar is the food yeast feeds on, but a dough does not actually need sugar for the yeast to have a food source. When flour is hydrated, the starches break down into simple sugars, which the yeast can then use for food.

When yeast is put into a dough, it wakes up and begins feeding, creating carbon dioxide gas and alcohol. This process is called fermentation, and it leavens and flavors the bread.

Yeast and Temperature

Yeast is very sensitive to temperature. Cold temperatures slow yeast activity down, warm temperatures speed yeast activity up, while hot temperatures will eventually kill the yeast. Yeast begins to die around 140°F/60°C.

If you are adding the yeast into the dry ingredients of your dough, you want to use liquids that are around 120–130°F/49–54°C. This will feel very warm, but not hot to the touch. If you are adding the yeast directly into the liquid (to proof the yeast), you want to keep the liquid temperature around 110–115°F/43–46°C.

Proofing Yeast (Making Sure Your Yeast is Alive)

Proofing yeast is a process of adding dry yeast to warm liquid with a pinch of sugar. The liquid hydrates the yeast to wake it up, and the sugar gives the yeast a food source to begin feeding on. If the yeast is alive, you will start seeing little bubbles and foaming in the mixture. This is a way to make sure the yeast is alive and gives it a jump start so it is very active when it is added into your recipe.

While many recipes call for this step, it is never required. The original form of active dry yeast required the yeast to be hydrated to function properly in a dough. However, these days it is formulated in a way that doesn't require hydration before adding it to your dough. If your recipe does not call for this step, you can still do it with the following process, prior to mixing your other ingredients, if you want to make sure your yeast is alive.

How to Proof Yeast

1. Warm about ½ cup (120 milliliters) of the liquid called for in the recipe to 110–115°F/43–46°C, which is just barely warmer than body temperature.
2. Add about ½ teaspoon of sugar and the yeast to the liquid. Stir it all together and wait about 5–10 minutes.
3. The yeast mixture should begin foaming and bubbling up. If you do not see foaming, then you need to get some new yeast. If you do see foaming, use the yeast in your recipe immediately.

> **Salt and Yeast:** It is a common misconception that you need to be careful about salt coming into close contact with the yeast in a bread dough. Salt will not kill the yeast in your recipe unless present in extremely high quantities.

The Stages of Making Bread

All bread recipes in this book will be made with the mixing method known as the Straight Dough Method. This means that, during the mixing step, all of the ingredients are mixed together all at once, with the exception of proofing the yeast first if desired. It is very simple and takes a lot of the stress out of baking bread.

Since this mixing method is so simple, I want to focus more on the stages the dough goes through from start to finish. A variety of other mixing methods are utilized when making more advanced breads, but all bread dough essentially goes through the same stages. Gaining an understanding of these stages is essential for building your bread-baking confidence.

Stage 1: Mixing

The ingredients are combined according to the recipe. At this stage, the goal is to simply make sure the ingredients are all together and a dough is starting to form. I like to use my hands during this stage and squeeze and pinch the dough all over to make sure all of the flour is thoroughly hydrated.

Stage 2: Building Gluten Structure

Once the ingredients are combined, it is important to build a strong gluten structure to capture the gases that the yeast creates. If your dough does not have a strong gluten structure, the gases will simply release out of the dough, instead of being trapped inside.

Gluten will form in a dough naturally, given enough time. This is why no-knead bread recipes work, because time is the element building strength in the dough. However, kneading the dough is the other main way that gluten structure is built in yeast bread. This method builds a stronger gluten structure quicker, which allows breads to be made with more yeast in the dough and shorter rising times.

How to Knead Dough by Hand

1. Turn the dough out onto a lightly floured clean work surface and gather it into a ball. Lightly flour the top of the dough.

2. Use the heel of your hand to push the dough away from you, focusing your pressure on going across the dough, rather than down into the table.

3. Fold the dough in half, bringing it back toward you.

4. Continue pushing the dough away from you, bringing it back toward you, and rotating it. This takes some practice to get into a rhythm.

5. If the dough is sticking to your table and your hands too much, you can add a bit more flour. However, you want the dough to stay soft and sticky to the touch. The dough will become less sticky and more elastic as you knead it.

6. Knead by hand until the dough is very smooth and elastic, and will stand up tall when rounded into a ball. This typically takes around 8–10 minutes. Take breaks if you need to.

Using a Mixer to Knead Dough

You can use a stand mixer to knead dough if you prefer.

1. Once the dough is mixed, turn the mixer, fitted with a dough hook, on to medium speed for 3 minutes.

2. Stop the mixer and scrape down the sides and the bottom of the bowl. If the dough is extremely sticky and is clinging to the sides of the bowl while it is running, add a bit more flour.

3. Turn the mixer back on medium speed for another 4–5 minutes.

4. The dough is finished when it is smooth and elastic and is clearing the sides of the bowl.

Stage 3: Bulk Fermentation

The bulk fermentation stage is the first rise the dough goes through as the yeast feeds on the available food. This develops flavor and continues building strength and structure in the dough.

The length of the bulk fermentation stage will vary widely, based on how much yeast is in the recipe, whether you used active dry or instant yeast, and how warm or cool your room temperature is.

Dough can move from the bulk fermentation phase into shaping once it is full of air and at least double in size. Some recipes may call for you to "punch" the air out of the dough and let it continue rising for a second time before shaping. This is still part of the bulk fermentation stage.

Stage 4: Degassing

Before shaping the dough, the recipe typically calls for it to be degassed or "punched down." There is no need to be aggressive with this step. Simply press down in the middle of the dough and bring the edges in to release the gas. This will allow for your shaped dough to have an even crumb after it rises again.

Stage 5: Shaping

Shaping is an important step in the bread-baking process, as it builds tension on the outside of the dough, which helps it to rise up instead of only spreading out. Several shaping techniques are covered later in the chapter with each master recipe.

Stage 6: Proofing

After the dough is shaped, it needs to rise one more time before going into the oven. This is called "proofing" or "proving." The amount of time this takes can vary widely. A small piece of dough (like a dinner roll) will proof much faster than a large loaf of bread. The process will also be slower or faster depending on the ambient temperature.

To know when your dough is ready to go into the oven, take a floured finger and gently press into the dough about ½ inch. If the hole fills in immediately, then it needs more time. If the hole fills in slowly (about 2–3 seconds), then it is ready to bake. If the dough feels like it might collapse when you press on it or the hole does not fill in, then it is over-proofed and is losing its structural integrity. You can still bake it, but it will likely deflate in the oven. Unfortunately, there is no coming back from over-proofing your dough, so it is important to keep an eye on it.

Stage 7: Baking

Bake your bread according to your specific recipe instructions. To know when your bread is fully cooked, it should sound hollow when thumped. You can also check the internal temperature with a digital thermometer. Bread is fully baked when the internal temperature reaches 190–200°F/87°–93°C.

Controlling the Speed of Your Dough

Temperature is the number one factor that will speed up or slow down the timeline of your dough. Knowing this, you can do a few things to help your dough better fit your schedule.

It is important to note that yeast dough that ferments quickly will have less flavor than yeast dough that ferments slowly. If you have the time, it is best not to rush it.

To Speed up Your Dough

If you need things to *move a little faster*, keep your dough in a warm environment. You can create a home proofer by placing the dough in your oven, powered off with the oven light on. Boil a pan of water and then place that pan on the rack underneath the dough and shut the oven door. Do not cover the dough when you do this. The warm and moist atmosphere will prevent it from drying out.

To Slow down Your Dough

You can utilize an optional step called "retarding," where you place the dough in the refrigerator to slow the progress. This not only puts a pause on the timeline of your dough, but it also increases the flavor of your final bread.

There are two points in the process at which you can retard your dough: *during bulk fermentation* and *during proofing*. After it's kneaded, you can place your dough in the refrigerator during the bulk-ferment phase for up to several days. All master recipes in this book work well for up to 3 days after kneading.

You can also place your dough in the refrigerator after it has been shaped. Recipes in this book can go for 16 hours in the refrigerator after shaping. The timeline for shaped dough is shorter because you can risk over-proofing your dough if you leave it too long.

In both cases, remove the dough from the refrigerator about 1½–2 hours before either shaping or baking. This is a great way to prep dough in the morning before work to bake fresh for dinner, or to prep cinnamon rolls the night before to bake them for breakfast the next morning.

Types of Yeast Dough

There are two main categories of yeasted dough: **lean dough** and **enriched dough**. Lean doughs do not contain any fat (or contain very little fat) while enriched doughs have a high ratio of fat added to them as well as things like sugar, eggs, and milk.

Lean dough creates breads that are typically crusty on the outside and very chewy in the middle. Things like baguette, ciabatta, pizza crust, and crusty artisan-style breads are all made from lean dough. Enriched doughs create breads that are much softer and more tender in texture due to the fat. Breads made from enriched doughs include soft dinner rolls, cinnamon rolls, brioche, challah, and yeasted donuts.

Sandwich breads are made from lean doughs or enriched doughs, depending on the final texture the recipe is aiming to achieve. A very soft and fluffy white bread is made from a slightly enriched bread, while a whole-grain bread like rye bread is typically made from a lean dough.

We're going to work from three master recipes in this chapter: A no-knead lean dough, a slightly enriched dough for sandwich bread, and a butter and egg enriched dough. These three doughs can create a wide variety of breads and being able to master them will really help you gain confidence in bread baking.

Using Whole Wheat Flour in Your Yeast Dough

Whole wheat flour can be used in place of some of the white flour in your yeast dough recipe. Whole wheat flour adds more flavor and more nutrients, so it can be desirable; however, it can also make a more dense and heavy bread.

I recommend substituting only up to half the total amount of white flour with whole wheat flour in a basic bread recipe. You can make bread with a higher ratio of whole wheat flour, but it requires more advanced bread techniques.

Rustic Boule (page 236)

NO-KNEAD LEAN DOUGH MASTER RECIPE

Yield: 1 boule, two 12-inch (30-cm) pizzas, or a 9 x 13-inch (23 x 33-cm) focaccia

Mixing Method: Straight Dough Method

- 420 grams (3½ cups) unbleached all-purpose flour or bread flour
- 9 grams (1¾ teaspoon) kosher salt
- ½ teaspoon instant yeast or ¾ teaspoon active dry yeast
- 28 grams (2 tablespoons) olive oil, *optional*
- 302 grams (1⅓ cup, 320 milliliters) water at about 120–130°F/49–54°C

If you have never baked a loaf of bread before, I encourage you to start here. No-knead bread is no-fuss and takes all of the intimidation out of working with yeast. The most common thing I use this dough for is a rustic boule (round loaf); however, it is also the dough I use for pizza crust, and it makes a beautiful focaccia with very little effort. You can use bread flour or unbleached all-purpose flour for this recipe. Bread flour will give you a stronger gluten structure and more rise out of your bread. The optional olive oil in the recipe will produce a bread that is slightly softer and less chewy than when it is left out.

Method

1. In a large mixing bowl, add all of the ingredients and stir to combine. Use your hands to squeeze and pinch the dough all over until all of the flour is fully hydrated.

2. Cover the bowl with plastic wrap (or a shower cap works really well) and let bulk-ferment at room temperature for 3½ hours. It is ready to be used once it is at least double in size and bubbly on top.

3. Shape, proof, and bake according to your desired use (details follow).

To Make a Rustic Boule

Specialty Equipment: Dutch oven or oven-safe pot at least 3 quarts in size
Prep Time: 20 minutes
Rising Time: 4 hours 30 minutes
Baking Time: 50 minutes
Total Time: 5 hours 40 minutes

1. Make the dough without the oil. Let it bulk-ferment.
2. Using a damp hand, scoop your hand underneath the dough, pulling up on a section, and fold it down over the top of the dough.
3. Continue doing this all the way around the bowl until the dough is formed into a tight ball. Pinch to seal the seam.
4. Dust a piece of parchment paper with cornmeal or flour. Dust the dough and your hands with flour. Transfer the dough, seam side down, to the parchment. Dust more flour over the top, cover with plastic wrap, and let proof for 45 minutes to 1 hour until puffy and full of air.
5. 30 minutes into the proofing time, position an oven rack in the center position and place a Dutch oven or oven-safe pot with a lid inside. Preheat to 450°F/230°C.
6. Carefully transfer the dough on the parchment into the preheated pot and cover with the lid.
7. Bake at 450°F/230°C covered for 30 minutes. Remove the lid and bake for another 10–20 minutes until the crust of the bread reaches a deep golden brown.
8. Let cool on a cooling rack for at least 1 hour before slicing.
9. Store uneaten bread cut-side-down on a cutting board in the open air for up to 2 days. Then slice and transfer to the freezer for storing up to 3 months.

To Make Focaccia Bread

Specialty Equipment: 9 x 13-inch (23 x 33-cm) metal baking pan
Prep Time: 20 minutes
Rising Time: 6 hours 30 minutes
Cook Time: 30 minutes
Total Time: 7 hours 20 minutes

1. Make the dough with the oil in the recipe. Let bulk-ferment.
2. After the dough is finished bulking, liberally oil a 9 x 13-inch (23 x 33-cm) metal baking pan with olive oil (about 2 tablespoons). Place the dough in the pan and turn to coat.
3. Gently stretch the dough until it fills the pan as much as possible. It may not want to stretch all the way to the corners at this point.
4. Cover the pan with plastic wrap and let rise for 2–3 hours until full of air. *(Note: to make this bread fit my schedule, I will often put it in the refrigerator right after bulk and then let it proof at room temperature the next day before baking.)*
5. Use your fingertips to dimple the dough all over while also stretching it to fit the pan. Drizzle a little more olive oil over the top and sprinkle toppings over the dough, like flaky salt, fresh herbs, olives, or cheese, if desired.
6. Bake at 425°F/220°C for 25–30 minutes until golden brown.
7. Transfer the focaccia to a cutting board to cut and serve.
8. Store uneaten focaccia in a zip-top bag at room temperature for up to 2 days, or in the freezer for up to 3 months.

To Make a Pizza Crust

Specialty Equipment: Pizza peel or pizza pan, pizza stone (optional)
Prep Time: 30 minutes
Rise Time: 4 hours
Bake Time: 15 minutes
Total Time: 4 hours 45 minutes

1. Make the dough with the oil. Let bulk-ferment.

2. Turn the dough out onto a lightly floured work surface and divide into two equal pieces. Round each piece into a ball. Cover and let rest for 30 minutes.

3. Meanwhile, prepare the oven. Place a baking stone or two sheet pans stacked together and turned upside down on the center rack. Preheat the oven to as high as your oven will allow. You want the surface to be as hot as possible when your pizza goes in.

4. Lightly flour the top of a piece of dough and press down on the dough with your fingertips to flatten it into a circular shape, leaving a small lip all around the edge for a crust.

5. Pick up the dough and use the backs of your hands and gravity to stretch the dough, turning it as you go. Focus on placing your hands in sections that are thicker to allow the dough to stretch evenly.

6. Once your dough is stretched to about 12 inches (30 cm) wide, transfer it to a cutting board or pizza peel that has been dusted liberally with cornmeal. Alternatively, you can use a specialty pizza pan that has vent holes in the bottom.

7. Top the dough with your desired sauce and toppings. Do not overload it, or it won't be easy to transfer into the oven.

8. Slide the pizza onto the preheated pizza stone or baking sheet (or keep it on the pizza pan) and let bake until the crust is a deep golden brown. This will take anywhere from 7–15 minutes, depending on your oven. Keep the oven door shut as much as possible and watch through the window to monitor doneness.

Baker Bettie's Better Baking Book

SOFT SANDWICH BREAD MASTER RECIPE

Yield: 2 loaves

Special Equipment: Two 8.5 x 4.5-inch (22 x 11-cm) loaf pans

Mixing Method: Straight Dough Method

Prep Time: 25 minutes

Rising Time: 2 hours for instant yeast/4 hours for active dry yeast

Cook Time: 45 minutes

Total Time: 3 hours 10 minutes for instant yeast/5 hours 10 minutes for active dry yeast

- 114 grams (½ cup, 120 milliliters) water
- 454 grams (2 cups, 480 milliliters) milk
- 7 grams (2¼ teaspoons, 1 package) active dry or instant yeast
- 50 grams (¼ cup) granulated sugar
- 85 grams (6 tablespoons) unsalted butter, softened
- 15 grams (1 tablespoon) kosher salt
- 780–900 grams (6½–7½ cups) bread flour or unbleached all-purpose flour

This dough makes beautifully fluffy sandwich bread. It is a slightly enriched dough with the inclusion of milk and some butter. But it is still lean enough that the bread has a good balance of chewiness while still being soft. See the flavor variation section to see how this dough can be made into a wheat bread or a seeded loaf.

Method

1. Combine the water and milk and warm to about 110–115°F/43–46°C.
2. In a large mixing bowl, combine the warm liquid, yeast, and ½ teaspoon of the sugar. Stir to combine. Let this mixture sit for about 5–10 minutes until you see some bubbles and foaming.
3. Add the butter, the rest of the sugar, salt, and 780 grams (6 ½ cups) of the flour to the bowl. Use clean hands to mix until all the flour is hydrated and the ingredients are well incorporated. At this point the dough will likely be very sticky and shaggy.
4. **If kneading the dough by hand**, lightly dust a work surface with flour and turn the dough out onto it. Dust flour over the top of the dough and begin kneading it. Add a bit more flour as needed, up to 1 more cup. The dough should feel soft and sticky, but it shouldn't be gluing itself to the counter or your hands. Kneading by hand will take about 8–10 minutes. **If kneading with a stand mixer**, fit the mixer with the dough hook and knead it on medium-high speed. Add more flour bit by bit to the stand mixer until the dough pulls away from the sides of the bowl. If kneading in the stand mixer, knead for 6–8 minutes. When the dough is smooth and elastic and springs back when a finger is pressed into it, you are done kneading.
5. Grease a clean bowl with a bit of oil or non-stick spray and transfer your dough to the bowl, turning to coat. Cover the dough with a piece

of plastic wrap, or a shower cap, and let rise at room temperature until doubled in size. This will take about 1 hour if using instant yeast and 2 hours if using active dry yeast.

6. Grease two 8.5 x 4.5-inch (22 x 11-cm) loaf pans. Turn the dough out onto the lightly floured surface and lightly push the air out of the dough with the palm of your hand. Cut the dough into two equal pieces.

7. Gently pat each piece of dough into a rectangle (about the shape of the loaf pan). Tightly form each piece of dough into a loaf. See images for demonstration.

8. Place the formed loaves into the pans, seam side down, and gently press down on them with the palm of your hand to ensure they evenly fill the pan. Cover the shaped dough and let proof at room temperature until the loaves are beginning to crown the pan. This will take about 1 hour for rapid-rise yeast and 2 hours for active dry yeast.

9. Position an oven rack to the center position. Preheat the oven to 350°F/175°C.

10. Bake for 35–45 minutes until golden brown. The center of the loaves should read 190–200°F/88–93°C when fully baked.

11. Let cool on baking racks for at least 1 hour before slicing with a serrated knife.

12. Store cooled bread in a plastic bag at room temperature for 4 days. Alternatively, you can slice the loaves and place them in the freezer in a freezer bag. Toast to refresh. Refrigerating bread will cause it to stale more quickly.

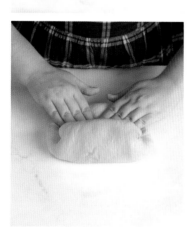

Baker Bettie's Better Baking Book

Flavor Variation Ideas

♦ **Honey Whole Wheat Sandwich Bread:** Replace the sugar in the recipe with 64 grams (3 tablespoons) honey. Reduce the white flour in the recipe to 540 grams (4 ½ cups) and add 210 grams (1¾ cups) whole wheat flour. When kneading, use more white flour if needed.

♦ **Seeded Sandwich Bread:** Reduce the white flour in the recipe to 540 grams (4 ½ cups) and add 210 grams (1¾ cup) whole wheat flour, 15 grams (2 tablespoons) sesame seeds, 30 grams (2 tablespoons) sunflower seeds, 10 grams (2 tablespoons) flaxseed or flax meal, and 25 grams (¼ cup) rolled oats to the dough. When kneading, use more white flour if needed. Top with a few rolled oats before baking if desired.

Sticky Buns (page 247)
Components: Enriched Yeast Dough (page 245), Caramel Sauce (page 251)

ENRICHED DOUGH MASTER RECIPE

Yield: 12 dinner rolls, cinnamon rolls, or sticky buns

Mixing Method: Straight Dough Method

- 7 grams (1 package, 2¼ teaspoon) active dry or instant yeast
- 227 grams (1 cup, 240 milliliters) whole milk (lower fat or non-dairy can be substituted)
- 50 grams (¼ cup) granulated sugar
- 480–600 grams (4–5 cups) all-purpose flour
- 7 grams (1½ teaspoons) kosher salt or table salt
- 85 grams (6 tablespoons) unsalted butter, very soft
- 2 large eggs, room temperature

This is my favorite dough to use for so many different breads. It is more heavily enriched with butter, eggs, and sugar, which makes for a very soft dough. I use it for dinner rolls, cinnamon rolls, sticky buns, and any other sweet-filled breads I want to make. It creates a soft and fluffy bread that is still slightly chewy.

Method

1. Warm the milk to about 110–115°F/43–46°C. In a large mixing bowl, add the warm milk, the yeast, and ½ teaspoon of sugar and stir to combine. Let sit for 5–10 minutes until you see some bubbles and foaming.

2. Add 480 grams (4 cups) of flour and the rest of the sugar, salt, butter, and eggs to the mixing bowl. Use clean hands to mix together until a sticky dough forms.

3. **If kneading by hand,** turn the dough out onto a floured countertop. Dust flour over the top of the dough and knead by hand for about 8–10 minutes until smooth and elastic. **If kneading with a stand mixer,** fit the mixer with a dough hook and knead at medium speed for 6–8 minutes. Add more flour as needed while kneading the dough. When the dough is finished being kneaded, it will still be slightly sticky to the touch, but it will feel smooth and elastic, and should stand tall when rounded into a ball.

4. Move the kneaded dough to a lightly oiled bowl, turn to coat, and cover with a piece of plastic wrap, a damp cloth, or a shower cap (my preference) to bulk-ferment until doubled in size, about 1 hour for rapid-rise yeast and 2 hours for active dry yeast.

5. Shape, proof, and bake according to your desired use.

To Make Filled Rolls

Yield: 12 rolls

Prep Time: 30 minutes

Rising Time: 1 hour 45 minutes for instant yeast/3 hours 15 minutes for active dry yeast

Cook Time: 35 minutes

Total Time: 2 hours 50 minutes for instant yeast/4 hours 20 minutes for active dry yeast

1. Make the dough and let it proof.
2. After bulk fermentation, turn the dough out onto a lightly floured countertop and roll it out into a rectangle about 18 x 12 inches (46 x 30 cm) in size.
3. Melt 56 grams (2 ounces, ½ stick) butter. Brush the dough with melted butter and add your filling of choice, leaving about ½ inch of the dough free from filling at the bottom long edge.
4. Starting on the long edge that does have filling, tightly roll the dough up into a log. Pinch the clean edge to the log to seal.
5. Use a serrated knife to divide the dough into 4 equal pieces.
6. Now cut each quarter of the log into 3 equal pieces to get 12 rolls.
7. Transfer the cut rolls into a greased 9 x 13-inch (23 x 33-cm) baking dish and cover with plastic wrap.
8. Proof the rolls for about 45 minutes if using instant yeast and about 75 minutes if using active dry yeast.
9. Position an oven rack to the center position. Preheat the oven to 350°F/175°C.
10. Bake for 30–35 minutes, until golden brown.

Baker Bettie's Better Baking Book

Flavor Variation Ideas

♦ **Cinnamon Rolls:** Combine 200 grams (1 cup) dark brown sugar with 3 tablespoons cinnamon for the filling. While rolls are still warm, frost with cream cheese frosting (page 177).

♦ **Sticky Buns:** Make caramel sauce (page 251). Pour the sauce into your prepared pan and top with 200 grams (about 2 cups) roughly chopped pecans. Combine 200 grams (1 cup) dark brown sugar with 2 teaspoons cinnamon and sprinkle over the dough for your filling. Set the cut rolls over the caramel/pecan mixture in your pan. As soon as the rolls are done baking, carefully flip the rolls out upside down on a serving platter, allowing the caramel/pecan mixture to become the topping.

To Make Dinner Rolls

Yield: 12 rolls
Prep Time: 30 minutes
Rising Time: 1 hour 45 minutes for instant yeast/3 hours 15 minutes for active dry yeast
Cook Time: 35 minutes
Total Time: 2 hours 50 minutes for instant yeast /4 hours 20 minutes for active dry yeast

1. Make the dough and let it proof.
2. After proofing, turn the dough out onto a lightly floured countertop and divide it into 12 equal pieces.
3. To shape the rolls, pull down on the sides of a piece of dough, creating a seam at the bottom.
4. Place the piece of dough, seam side down, on an un-floured part of the countertop. Cup your hand over the dough and roll it under your palm to form a smooth piece of dough.
5. Place the shaped rolls on a parchment-lined sheet pan, or in a 9 x 13-inch (23 x 33-cm) baking dish that has been lightly greased. Cover the rolls with plastic wrap.
6. Proof the rolls for about 45 minutes if using instant yeast and about 75 minutes if using active dry yeast.
7. Position an oven rack to the center position. Preheat the oven to 375°F/190°C.
8. Brush with an egg wash (page 255). Bake for 15–20 minutes, until golden brown. If desired, brush baked rolls with melted butter and sprinkle with flaky salt.

Salted Caramel Pecan Brownies (page 124)
Components: Classic Brownie Recipe (page 123), Caramel Sauce (page 251)

10

Miscellaneous Techniques & Components

BERRY SAUCE

Yield: 2 cups (480 milliliters)
Prep Time: 5 minutes
Cook Time: 5 minutes
Total Time: 10 minutes

- 28 grams (2 tablespoons) water
- 28 grams (2 tablespoons) lemon, lime, or orange juice
- 8 grams (1 tablespoon) cornstarch
- 50 grams (¼ cup) sugar
- 450 grams (1 pound) fresh berries (strawberries, blueberries, raspberries, or cranberries)
- 1 teaspoon lemon, lime, or orange zest

This berry sauce can be made with any berry you like, or a combination of a few. Serve over cheesecake or angel food cake, or with strawberry shortcake.

Method

1. In a medium saucepan, add the water, juice, cornstarch, and sugar, and whisk to combine.
2. Add the fresh fruit to the pan. If using strawberries, hull and quarter them first.
3. Cook over medium heat, stirring frequently, for about 4–5 minutes until the liquid is rapidly bubbling.
4. Remove from the heat, stir in the zest, and let cool before serving. The liquid will thicken as it cools.
5. Store in an airtight container in the refrigerator for up to 3 days.

CARAMEL SAUCE

Yield: About 1 ⅓ cups
(320 milliliters)
Prep Time: 5 minutes
Cook Time: 10 minutes
Total Time: 15 minutes

- 200 grams (1 cup) granulated sugar
- 120 grams (½ cup, 120 milliliters) water
- 235 grams (1 cup, 240 milliliters) heavy cream
- 2 grams (½ teaspoon) kosher salt

I think many people are surprised at how simple it is to make a homemade caramel sauce. Serve over ice cream, drizzled in between cake layers, over a slice of apple pie, or simply dip apple slices in it.

Method

1. In a saucepan at least 3 quarts in size, add the sugar and pour the water over the sugar, being careful not to splash sugar granules up the side of the pan.

2. Turn the heat on to medium. The sugar will start to dissolve in the water and will come to a boil. As the mixture boils, the sugar will start caramelizing. Stay close by because the caramelization process moves very quickly. Do not stir during this process, or you risk re-crystallizing the sugar, resulting in a gritty texture. If the sugar is caramelizing unevenly, gently swirl the pan to even out the color.

3. Once the sugar smells nutty and is golden brown, carefully pour all of the heavy cream into the pan and stir vigorously with a silicone spatula. The mixture will bubble up quite a bit.

4. Add the salt and continue cooking and stirring the mixture until it thickens, about 3–5 minutes.

5. Remove the sauce from the heat and pour into a heat-resistant container. A mason jar is perfect. Store in the refrigerator for up to 1 month.

Chocolate Cupcakes (page 149) with Ganache Glaze

CHOCOLATE GANACHE

2:1 Ganache Ratio (for Truffles)

- 225 grams (8 ounces) bittersweet or semi-sweet chocolate
- 118 grams (½ cup) heavy cream, whipping cream, or double cream
- ¼ teaspoon kosher salt

1:1 Ganache Ratio (for frosting, whipped ganache, or filling a cake)

Small Batch (for cake glaze)

- 113 grams (4 ounces) bittersweet or semi-sweet chocolate
- 118 grams (½ cup) heavy cream, whipping cream, or double cream
- pinch of salt

Medium Batch (for filling a cake or to frost 12 cupcakes)

- 227 grams (8 ounces) bittersweet or semi-sweet chocolate
- 235 grams (1 cup) heavy cream, whipping cream, or double cream
- ¼ teaspoon kosher salt

Large Batch (for frosting 24 cupcakes or a layer cake)

- 454 grams (1 pound) bittersweet or semi-sweet chocolate
- 470 grams (2 cups) heavy cream, whipping cream, or double cream
- 2 grams (½ teaspoon) kosher salt

Chocolate ganache is a simple mixture of chocolate and cream that has a wide variety of uses. It can be made into truffles or whipped chocolate frosting, or used to fill a cake, or to make a rich glaze. Depending on your intended use for the ganache, you can change the ratio of chocolate to cream for your desired consistency.

Method

1. Chop the chocolate up into small pieces and place in a large mixing bowl. Alternatively, you can use chocolate chips.

2. Heat the cream in a saucepan over medium heat until it is simmering.

3. Pour the hot cream over the chocolate and let stand for 5 minutes. Add the salt.

4. Put the whisk directly in the center of the chocolate/cream mixture and begin whisking in small circles, slowly moving outward in bigger circles until the mixture is smooth.

5. If not using immediately, place a piece of plastic wrap directly touching the ganache so a hard skin does not form. Ganache can remain at room temperature for 48 hours, and then it should be refrigerated. Keep in mind that it will firm up considerably in the refrigerator and will likely need to come back to room temperature before using.

To Make Ganache Frosting or Whipped Ganache

1. Make the medium or large batch of 1:1 ganache.

2. Allow to come to room temperature naturally (will take several hours) or place in the refrigerator for about 1 hour, until the consistency of pudding.

3. You can use it as is to frost or fill a cake. It also works well for piping on cupcakes. To *make a whipped ganache frosting*, whip with the whisk attachment of your stand mixer or a hand mixer until light and fluffy.

To Make a Cake Glaze

1. Make the small batch 1:1 ganache.
2. While still warm, drizzle over your cake.

To Make Truffles

1. Make the 2:1 ratio ganache.
2. Allow to come to room temperature naturally (will take several hours) or place in the refrigerator for about 1 hour, until firm enough to scoop.
3. Scoop about 1-tablespoon portions of firm ganache. Roll each portion between your palms and then roll it in your desired toppings. Rolling in cocoa powder is the most traditional, but you can roll them in sprinkles, chopped nuts, or coconut if you like.
4. If not serving immediately, store in an airtight container in the refrigerator for up to 1 week or in the freezer for up to 1 month.

Truffles with various toppings (cocoa powder, sprinkles, coconut, ground pecans, ground pistachios)

EGG WASH

Yield: ¼ cup (60 milliliters)
Total Time: 2 minutes

- 1 large egg
- 14 grams (1 tablespoon) water

An egg wash is a simple mixture of egg and water that can be brushed on top of pastries and breads before baking. This gives the final baked goods a shiny golden-brown finish.

Method

1. Combine the egg and water together and whisk vigorously until well combined and very smooth.
2. Brush on top of your baked goods before baking.

FRUIT GLAZE

Yield: 1 cup (240 milliliters)
Prep Time: 3 minutes
Cook Time: 2 minutes
Total Time: 5 minutes

- 280 grams (1 cup) apricot jelly or jam
- 28 grams (2 tablespoons) water

A basic fruit glaze is commonly used to finish the tops of fruit tarts or any other pastries that have fresh fruit on top. This gives the fruit a glossy finish.

Method

1. Combine the jelly or jam and water in a small saucepan over medium heat. Heat and stir until the mixture becomes loose.
2. If you used jam, strain the mixture through a fine mesh sieve to remove any lumps or seeds.
3. Let the mixture cool slightly. Brush gently over the fruit. Alternatively, you can toss the fruit in the glaze before topping the pastry.

TOASTED NUTS *or* COCONUT

Prep Time: 2 minutes

Cook Time: 4 minutes for stovetop/15 minutes for oven

Total Time: 6 minutes for stovetop/17 minutes for oven

- nut of choice, or sweetened or unsweetened flaked coconut, any quantity

I highly suggest toasting your nuts before adding them to your baked goods, unless they will be sitting right on top and will naturally toast during the baking process. Toasting brings out the natural oils in the nuts and makes them much crisper and more flavorful in texture. This method can also be used for coconut if you want a nuttier flavor. You can use this for any recipe that calls for nuts or coconut.

Method

Stovetop Method *(best for up to 2 cups)*
1. Pour the nuts or coconut into a dry skillet wide enough to allow them to be spread in a thin layer on the bottom of the pan.
2. Heat over medium-low heat, stirring frequently, until the nuts or coconut smell fragrant and nutty. This will take about 3–4 minutes.

Oven Method *(best for more than 2 cups)*:
1. Place the nuts or coconut on a sheet pan and spread into a thin even layer.
2. Toast in the oven at 325°F/165°F, stirring about every 4–5 minutes.
3. Remove from the oven when the nuts or coconut smells nutty or very fragrant. This should take about 10–15 minutes.
4. Store cooled nuts or coconut in an airtight container at room temperature for up to 1 month.

POWDERED SUGAR GLAZE

Yield: About ¼ cup—enough for a batch of muffins, scones, a sweet batter bread loaf, or a Bundt cake

Prep Time: 5 minutes

Total Time: 5 minutes

- 120 grams (1 cup) powdered, confectioner's, or icing sugar
- extracts, spices, or zests as desired
- pinch of salt
- 28–43 grams (2–3 tablespoons) liquid of choice

Powdered sugar glaze, also known as flat icing, is an incredibly quick and versatile topping to drizzle over muffins, batter breads, scones, and cakes. It is a simple mixture of powdered sugar and your liquid of choice to create any flavor you like.

Method

1. Place the powdered sugar in a small mixing bowl with the salt, zests, or extracts you are using.
2. Add the liquid into the bowl bit by bit, whisking until you have a thick glaze, about the consistency of honey. It should flow slowly off the whisk in a steady stream. If the glaze gets too thin, you can add a bit more powdered sugar to thicken it back up.
3. Store in an airtight container in the refrigerator for up to 1 week. Allow to come back to room temperature and re-whisk before drizzling.

Flavoring Your Glaze

You can flavor your glaze in a variety of ways. For a plain glaze or a glaze flavored with an extract like vanilla or almond extract, choose milk as your liquid. Or you can opt to use a fruit juice like lemon or orange to make a fruit-flavored glaze.

Extracts & Zests
(Use 1–2 if desired)

- 1 teaspoon vanilla extract
- ¼ teaspoon almond extract
- ¼ teaspoon anise extract
- ¼ teaspoon mint extract
- 1 tablespoon orange, lemon, or lime zest

Spices
(Use 1–2 if desired)

- ½ teaspoon cinnamon
- ½ teaspoon apple pie spice
- ½ teaspoon pumpkin pie spice
- pinch of nutmeg, allspice, and/or clove

Liquids

- Milk (for a plain glaze or for vanilla or almond glazes)
- Fruit juice: lemon, orange, lime, cranberry, apple cider, etc.

Flavor Variation Ideas

♦ **Citrus Glaze:** Use orange, lemon, or lime juice as the liquid. Add 1 tablespoon of corresponding orange, lemon, or lime zest.

♦ **Vanilla Glaze:** Use milk as the liquid and add ½ teaspoon of vanilla extract or vanilla paste.

♦ **Apple Cider Glaze:** Use apple cider or apple juice as the liquid and add ½ teaspoon of apple pie spice.

♦ **Almond Glaze:** Use milk as the liquid and add ¼ teaspoon of almond extract.

Lemon Poppyseed Muffins (page 90) with Lemon Glaze

Crumb Cake (page 156)
Components: Pound Cake (page 155), Streusel Topping (page 261)

STREUSEL TOPPING

Yield: About 1 ½ cups, enough for a 9-inch (23-cm) pie or cake, 1 batch of muffins, or a loaf of quick bread. Double the recipe for a 9 x 13-inch (23 x 33-cm) pan.

Prep Time: 5 minutes

Total Time: 5 minutes

- 100 grams (½ cup) brown sugar, light or dark
- 100 grams (½ cup) granulated sugar
- 75 grams (½ cup + 2 tablespoons) all-purpose flour
- 1 ½ teaspoons cinnamon
- pinch of salt
- 56 grams (4 tablespoons, ½ stick) unsalted butter, melted

Streusel is a crumbly mixture of flour, butter, and sugar. It often also has nuts and/or oats added to it as well. Streusel topping is most commonly used on fruit pies, a crisp, or a crumble, and should be added right before the pie goes into the oven. It can also be used to top muffins, batter breads, and cakes.

Method

1. In a medium bowl, whisk the flour, brown sugar, cinnamon, and salt together.

2. Stir in the melted butter and mix with your hands until crumbly.

Flavor Variation Ideas

- ◆ **Oat Streusel:** Add 50 grams (½ cup) rolled or quick oats to the mixture.

- ◆ **Nut Streusel:** Add 50 grams (½ cup) chopped nuts to the mixture.

WHIPPED CREAM TOPPING

Yield: About 2 cups, enough for a 9-inch (23-cm) pie

Specialty Equipment:
Hand mixer or stand mixer

Prep Time: 15 minutes

Total Time: 15 minutes

- 235 grams (1 cup, 240 milliliters) heavy cream or whipping cream, cold
- 40 grams (⅓ cup) powdered, confectioner's, or icing sugar

Whipped cream is the perfect topping for pound cake, angel food cake, shortcake, and cream pies!

Method

Prep:

1. It is important that the cream is very cold in order for it to whip up properly. If your kitchen is very warm, you may want to put the mixing bowl and your beaters in the freezer for a few minutes before starting.

To Make the Whipped Cream:

1. Place the cream in the bowl of a stand mixer fitted with a whisk attachment, or in a large mixing bowl with a hand mixer.

2. Begin whipping on medium speed until soft peaks begin to form.

3. With the mixer still running, slowly add the sugar and any extracts if using, and mix until medium peaks form. Be careful not to over-whip the cream. It will start looking curdled if you go too far, as it begins turning into butter.

4. Serve as soon as possible. If you want to serve it the next day, under-whip slightly and store in an airtight container in the refrigerator. Finish whipping right before serving.

Flavoring Whipped Cream

- **Vanilla Whipped Cream:** Add 1 teaspoon vanilla extract or vanilla bean paste.

- **Chocolate Whipped Cream:** Add 10 grams (2 tablespoons) cocoa powder in with the cream.

- **Almond Whipped Cream:** Add ½ teaspoon almond extract.

- **Cinnamon Whipped Cream:** Add 1 teaspoon cinnamon in with the cream.

- **Espresso Whipped Cream:** Add 1 teaspoon instant espresso in with the cream.

Baking Conversions

Weights for Common Baking Ingredients

Ingredient	Weight	Volume
Butter	227 grams	1 cup, 2 sticks
Buttermilk	240 grams	1 cup, 240 milliliters
Chocolate Chips	150 grams	1 cup
Cocoa Powder	80 grams	1 cup
Cornstarch	120 grams	1 cup
Cream, heavy or whipping	235 grams	1 cup, 240 milliliters
Cream Cheese	226 grams, 8 ounces	—
Eggs, whole without shell (large)	50 grams	—
Eggs, yolk only (large)	18 grams	—
Eggs, white only (large)	32 grams	—
Flour, all-purpose, bread, whole wheat	120 grams	1 cup
Flour, cake	115 grams	1 cup
Honey	340 grams	1 cup, 240 milliliters
Milk	227 grams	1 cup, 240 milliliters
Nuts, roughly chopped	100 grams	1 cup
Oats	100 grams	1 cup
Peanut Butter	254 grams	1 cup
Raisins	150 grams	1 cup
Shortening	192 grams	1 cup
Sour Cream	240 grams	1 cup
Sugar, light or dark brown, granulated (lightly packed)	200 grams	1 cup
Sugar, powdered	120 grams	1 cup
Water	227 grams	1 cup, 240 milliliters

Common Measurement Conversions

Teaspoons	Tablespoons	Milliliters
1 ½ teaspoons	½ tablespoon	8 milliliters
3 teaspoons	1 tablespoon	15 milliliters
6 teaspoons	2 tablespoons	30 milliliters

Tablespoons	Cups	Fluid Oz.	Milliliters
4 tablespoons	¼ cup	2 fluid oz.	60 milliliters
5 tablespoons + 1 teaspoon	⅓ cup	2 ⅔ fluid oz.	80 milliliters
8 tablespoons	½ cup	4 fluid oz.	120 milliliters
16 tablespoons	1 cup	8 fluid oz.	240 milliliters

Cups	Pints	Quarts	Gallons	Liters
2 cups	1 pint	½ quart	—	480 milliliters
4 cups	2 pints	1 quart	—	960 milliliters
16 cups	8 pints	4 quarts	1 gallon	1.9 liters

Temperature Conversions

Fahrenheit	Celsius	Gas Mark
250°F	120°C	½
275°F	135°C	1
300°F	150°C	2
325°F	165°C	3
350°F	175°C	4
375°F	190°C	5
400°F	205°C	6
425°F	220°C	7
450°F	230°C	8
475°F	250°C	9

Note: *If your oven is fan-assisted, as a general rule of thumb, you should heat it 25°F/15°C lower than the recipe states. Keep an eye on the baked good, as it still might bake faster due to the moving air.*

Acknowledgements

First and foremost, I need to thank the entire Baker Bettie community, whether you've been following my website for years, are part of the Facebook, Instagram, or YouTube communities, or if you just recently found me on TikTok! All of you are the reason I can teach baking for a living and why I was able to write this book. Thank you for being here!

To my mother and sister, thank you for your unending support. For never questioning all the forks in the road I've taken with my career. Thank you for always believing in me.

To my dear friend and assistant Kelly Haines: This book quite literally wouldn't have been possible without all of your assistance with recipe testing, food styling, and ongoing valued input. I am so grateful to have you as part of the Baker Bettie team.

I am so thankful to my editor Jane Kinney-Denning for convincing me I was capable of this project and for all of the guidance you and the entire Mango Publishing team have given me along the way. It has been so wonderful to work with all of you.

Thank you to Lindsey Nelmar, my incredibly generous neighbor and friend, for your valuable insight on the book from a reader's perspective.

I need to give a special thanks to the group of volunteer recipe testers for being so giving with your time and feedback. Your input on the recipes for this book was invaluable.

I am incredibly thankful to my dearest blogging friends, Laura Davidson, Melissa Belanger, Megan Hastings, and Lindsay Moe, for always lending an ear and words of encouragement. I love you all so much.

To Sally McKenney, I am so honored to have you write the foreword for the book. I have always looked up to you and admired your career. Thank you for being a part of this project.

Thank you to my dear friend Jessica Ellington for offering your expertise and consulting on the accuracy of the contents of the book.

And I can never say enough thanks to my incredible husband, Chris. Thank you for standing by my side during this project and every day. Thank you for reminding me that I'm capable and worthy. I love you more than I can express.

About the Author

Kristin "Baker Bettie" Hoffman is a trained chef, baking educator, and creator of the popular baking blog BakerBettie.com. Kristin's approach is to teach foundational recipes, baking techniques, and accessible baking science. She believes gaining an understanding of the "whys" of baking helps foster confidence in the kitchen. Her readers praise her ability to connect the dots between techniques and big picture concepts to show not only what to bake, but how to bake.

Kristin has an affinity for retro style and "Baker Bettie" is her public alter ego that brings a bit of nostalgia for the desserts and baked goods you might remember growing up with. Kristin wants the process of learning to bake to feel comforting and approachable, and she believes a warm retro feel helps with this. She teaches as Baker Bettie on her website, YouTube channel, and online baking school, The Better Baking School. She also hosts live workshops and corporate events in the Chicago area.

Index

A

All-purpose flour 31-34, 49, 89, 93, 97, 101, 107, 111, 115-116, 123, 127, 133, 139, 144, 149, 187, 203, 235, 241, 245, 261
Angel Food Cake 17, 146, 162-163, 165-166, 213, 250, 263
    Chocolate 166
Apple 14-15, 98, 182, 194-197, 222, 251, 258
    Pie, Dutch 182, 194, 222
    Spice Oat Bread/Muffins 98

B

Baking powder 33-34, 41-42, 72, 83, 89, 93, 97, 101, 107, 111, 127, 139, 149-150, 159, 171
Baking soda 41-42, 44-45, 48, 72, 83, 101, 107, 115, 123, 139, 149-150, 159, 171
Banana 47, 85, 97-98, 207, 221
    Muffins, Chocolate Chip 85, 97-98
    Cream Pie 221
Batter 19, 30, 41, 47, 49–60, 62-64, 66, 73, 75, 83-87, 89-91, 93-94, 97-99, 102, 124, 128, 150, 152, 155-156, 159-160, 163, 166, 168, 171-172, 257, 261
Berry sauce 250
Biscuits 17, 33, 36, 50, 61-62, 83, 103, 107-109, 193, 199
    Buttermilk 107-109, 199
    Drop 107, 109
    Fresh Herb 17, 109
    Garlic Cheddar 109
Bread, batter 60
    Apple Spice Oat Bread/Muffins 98
    Banana Bread/Muffins, Chocolate Chip 98
    Blueberry Coffee Cake Loaf/Muffins 90
    Carrot Bread/Muffins, Loaded 98
    Cheddar Dill Bread 94
    Lemon Poppy Seed Loaf/Muffins 90
    Master Recipe, Fruit or Veg 97-99
    Master Recipe, Savory 93-94
    Master Recipe, Sweet 89-91
    Parmesan Herb Bread 94
    Zucchini Bread/Muffins, Lemon 85, 97-98
Bread, yeast 31, 33-34, 41, 43, 47, 60, 62-65, 83-84, 225-230, 232-233, 235, 241-242, 245-247
    Cinnamon Rolls 177, 233, 245, 247
    Dinner rolls 233, 245, 247
    Enriched Dough Master Recipe 245-247
    Filled rolls 246
    Focaccia 235, 237
    Honey Whole Wheat Sandwich 243

    No-Knead Lean Dough 235
    Pizza 233, 235, 238
    Rustic boule 235-236
    Seeded Sandwich 243
    Soft Sandwich 241
    Stages of making 228
    Sticky Buns 245, 247
Blind baking 60, 62, 191, 200, 207-208, 211-212, 221-222
    About 60
    How to 191
Blondies 120, 127-128
    Funfetti 128, 160
    Master Recipe 127-128
    White Chocolate Walnut, Classic 128
Blueberry 83, 90, 113
    Blueberry Coffee Cake Loaf/Muffins 90
Brown sugar, light and dark 37-38, 42, 72-73, 98, 123, 127, 139-140, 197, 222, 247, 261
Brownies 60, 120, 123-124, 127
    Master Recipe, Classic Fudgy 123-124
    Salted Caramel Pecan 124
    Spiced Hot Chocolate 124
Bulk-ferment 60, 65, 230, 232, 235-238, 245-246
Butter 35-37, 43, 48, 50-51, 54, 59, 61-62, 66, 76, 85, 87, 101-104, 107-109, 111, 115-116, 120, 123-124, 127, 130-131, 133, 139-140, 152-153, 155, 159, 171, 173, 175-177, 185, 187-188, 193, 197-199, 207, 211, 213, 218, 222, 233, 241, 245-247, 261, 263
    Salted vs. unsalted 36
Buttercream 61, 135, 160, 173, 175-177, 217-218
    Berry 176
    Chocolate 176
    Citrus 176
    Coconut 60, 176
    Peanut Butter 176
    Vanilla 160, 175
Buttermilk 44, 48-49, 51, 94, 101, 107-108, 115-116, 171, 199
    Substitute 48-49

C

Cake 17, 30, 32-33, 40, 48-49, 55, 62, 90, 124, 143-179, 208, 211-213, 218, 250-251, 253-254, 257, 261, 263
    Angel Food 17, 146, 162-163, 165-166, 213, 250, 263
    Boston Cream Pie 172
    Coconut 160
    Funfetti 160
    Layer, how to build 178-179
    Lemon Rosemary
    Master Recipe, Classic Chocolate 149-150
    Master Recipe, Pound 155-156
    Pound -, Marble 156
    White -, Classic 159-160
    Yellow Chiffon 171-172
cake flour 32-33, 49, 144, 149, 155, 159, 165-166, 171
    Substitute 49
Caramel Sauce 124, 247, 251

Caramelize 60
Caster sugar 38
Cheesecake 48, 133, 193-194, 200, 203-205, 250
    Master Recipe 203-205
Chocolate 45, 51, 66, 73, 98, 119-120, 123-124, 127-128, 130, 139, 140, 145, 149-150, 156, 166, 176, 180, 182, 193, 207, 221, 253
    Banana Bread/Muffins, Chocolate Chip 98
    Buttercream 176
    Cake, Death by 150
    Cake, Classic 149-150
    Chip Pecan, Chewy 140
    Cream Pie 182, 221
    Ganache 150, 156, 172, 178, 182, 204, 253-254
    Monster Cookies 140
    Pastry Cream 182, 208, 221
Cinnamon Rolls 177, 233, 245-247
Cobbler 107, 184, 197, 199, 222
    About 184
    Fruit 199
    Peach 222
Cocoa powder 42, 45-46, 66, 72, 123-124, 141, 145, 149-150, 156, 166, 176, 208, 254, 263
    Blooming 124
    Dutch-processed 45-46, 141, 150, 166, 176
    Natural 34, 42, 45-46, 123-124, 141, 149-150, 166, 176
Coconut 91, 98, 113, 157, 160, 176-177, 207-208, 221, 254, 256
    Cake 160
    Cream Pie 207, 221
    Pastry Cream 182, 208, 221
Cookies 22, 47-48, 51, 56, 61-62, 119-120, 127, 130-131, 133-135, 139-141, 193-194
    Chocolate Chip Pecan, 140
    Drop 120, 130, 139-141
    Master Recipe, Drop 139-141
    Monster 140
    Master Recipe, Shortbread 133-136
    Oatmeal Raisin, Spiced Rum-Soaked 140
Cornbread 85, 101-102
    Jalapeno Cheddar 102
    Master Recipe 101-102
    Smoky Chipotle 102
Cream 41, 43-44, 50-51, 56, 64-65, 111-113, 153, 172, 175-176, 251, 253, 263
Creaming 35, 37, 50, 54, 61-62, 68, 120, 130-131, 133, 139-140, 144, 152-153, 155, 159, 173, 175
Crimp 61, 190-191, 198, 214
    About 61
    How to 190
Crumb 62, 84, 130, 136, 146, 155-156, 182, 184, 193, 200, 203, 208, 221, 231
    About 62
    Cake 156
Crust 50, 60-62, 65, 133, 136, 182, 184-185, 187-191 193-195, 197-198, 200, 203, 205, 207-208, 212-215, 218, 221-222, 233, 235, 238-239
    Cookie Crumb 182, 184, 193-195, 200, 203, 208, 221
    Pie Pastry, Traditional 182, 184, 187-189, 194, 200, 205, 208, 212, 221

Shortbread 133-136, 182, 184, 194, 203, 208, 212
Curd 41, 178 ,182, 204, 211-212, 222
    Cake filling 212
    Master Recipe 211
    Meringue Pie 212, 222
    Tart 212
Cut in 61, 103-105

D

Dairy products 44
Dock 62, 135-136, 191
Dough 30, 41, 43, 49-50, 55, 60-66, 73, 84, 93, 103-105, 107-109, 111-113,115-116, 130-131, 133-136, 139-141, 184-185, 187-188, 190, 194, 198-199, 213-215, 226-233, 235-238, 241-243, 245-247

E

Egg(s) 37, 39-41, 43, 47-48, 50-51, 62-64, 66, 89, 93, 97, 101, 104, 111, 120, 123, 127, 130-131, 139, 144, 146, 149, 153, 155, 159, 162-163, 165-166, 168-169, 171-172, 198, 200, 203, 207, 211, 213-215, 217, 233, 245, 247, 255
    Function of yolks 41
    Function of whites 40
    Function of whole eggs 39
    How to separate 40
    Sizing 39
    Wash 198, 214, 247, 255
    White vs. brown 39
Emulsion 41, 62-63, 130
Equipment 53-57, 76, 89, 93, 97, 101, 107, 111, 115, 123, 127, 133, 139, 149, 155, 159, 165, 171, 175, 177, 187, 193, 203, 207, 211, 217, 225, 236-238, 241, 263
    Baking pans 55
    Measuring 54
    Mixing 54
    Miscellaneous 55-56

F

Fat 34-37, 39-41, 43-44, 50, 61-62, 84-85, 103-105, 107, 111, 115, 120, 130, 146, 162, 168, 185, 187, 233
    Role in baking 35, 37
    Substituting solid and liquid fats 37
    Varieties of 35-37
Ferment 63, 226
Flour 30-35, 37, 47, 49-50, 61-62, 64, 66, 70-72, 84, 86, 89, 93, 97, 101, 103-105, 107-108, 111-112, 115-116, 123, 127, 133-134, 139, 141, 144-146, 149, 155-156, 159, 162, 165-166, 171, 185, 187-188, 203, 213, 226, 228-230, 235-236, 238, 241-243, 245, 261
    Bleached vs. unbleached 31
    Role in baking 30
    Varieties of 32-34

Whole wheat vs. white 30
Foaming methods 162
Folding 63, 75, 105,
Frosting 61, 135, 150, 160, 172-173, 175-179, 217, 247, 253
Buttercream 61, 135, 160, 173, 175-177, 217-218
Cream Cheese 135, 160, 172, 177, 247
Ganache, Whipped 150, 253
Fruit 41, 91, 94, 97-99, 113, 128, 141, 156-157, 178, 182, 184, 194, 197-199, 200, 204, 208, 211-213, 221-222, 250, 255, 257-258, 261
Cobbler 199
Crisp or Crumble 199
Curd Tart 212
Glaze 208, 255
Master Recipe, Curd 211-213
Master Recipe, Pie Filling 197-199
Pie, Traditional 198
Tart, Pastry Cream 208

G

Ganache 150, 156, 172, 178, 182, 204, 253-254
Gluten 30-35, 37, 47, 60-61, 63-64, 84-85, 103-105, 115, 123, 127, 144, 146, 185, 188, 228-229, 235
About 30, 64
Graham Cracker Crust 182, 193, 205
Granulated sugar 37-38, 89, 93, 97-98, 111-112, 115, 123, 127, 133, 135, 139-140, 149, 155, 159, 165, 171, 187, 193, 197, 203, 207, 211, 214, 217, 222, 241, 245, 251, 261

K

knead 30, 62, 64, 104-105, 115, 188, 229-230, 232, 241, 243, 245
By hand 104-105, 115, 188, 229-230, 241, 245
With mixer 230, 241, 245

L

Lard 36, 103, 107, 185
Lattice crust, how to 214-215
Leaven 35, 37, 40-44, 48, 61, 64, 130, 144, 146, 226
Leavening agents 41-44
Biological leavening 43
Chemical leavening 41-42, 83, 146
Physical leavening 43-44
Lemon 48-49, 89-90, 98-99, 113, 128, 134, 141, 157, 162, 165, 172, 176-177, 197-198, 203-204, 211, 222, 250, 257-258
Meringue Pie 222
Poppy Seed Loaf/Muffins 90
Rosemary Cake 172
Scones, Blueberry 113
Lining pans 87, 144-146
Round 145-146

Square or rectangular 87

M

Measuring 54-56, 66, 70-73, 75-77
By weight 71
By volume 72-73
Meringue 41, 63, 159, 162-163, 165, 173, 182, 212-213, 217-218, 222
Buttercream, Swiss 173, 213, 217-218
Mise en place 75-76, 168
Mixing methods
Angel Food Method 162-163
Biscuit Mixing Method 84, 103-105, 107, 111, 115, 185
Blending Method for Cakes 146, 149
Chiffon Mixing Method 162, 168, 171
Creaming Method for Cakes 152-153, 155, 159
Creaming Method for Cookies 130-131, 133, 139
Muffin Mixing Method 85-86, 89, 93, 97, 101
One-Bowl Method for Cookies 120, 123, 127, 140
Muffins (see bread, batter) 33, 38, 47, 60, 85-87, 89-90, 97-98, 101-102

O

Oil 36, 85, 87, 89, 93, 97, 149, 171, 235-238, 241

P

Pastry cream 41, 172, 178, 182, 205, 207-208, 213, 221
Cake filling 208
Chocolate 182, 208, 221
Coconut 208, 221
Master Recipe 207-208
Peanut Butter 208
Peaks 64-65, 162-163, 168-169, 213
Peanut butter 128, 140-141, 176, 208
Buttercream 176
Monster Cookies 140
Pastry Cream 208
Pie 36, 50, 60-62, 65, 136, 172, 181-222, 251, 258, 261, 263
Categories of 182, 184
Chocolate Cream 182, 221
Coconut Cream 207, 221
Dutch Apple 182, 194, 222
Fruit - Filling 197-199, 221-222
Fruit -, Traditional 198
Lemon Meringue 222
- Pastry, Traditional 182, 184-185, 187-188, 194, 200, 205, 208, 212, 221
Strawberry Rhubarb 222
Piping bag, how to fill 173
Pound cake 155-157, 263

Master Recipe 155-157
Marble 156
Powdered sugar 38, 66, 72, 91, 99, 111, 135-136, 173, 175-177, 212, 257, 263
    About 38
    Glaze 257-258
Proof (prove) 65, 226-227, 231, 233

Q

Quick breads (see also bread, batter) 83-116, 261
    About 83
    Mixing methods 84-87, 103-105

S

Salt 33-34, 36, 45, 89, 93, 97, 101, 107-109, 111, 115-124, 127, 133, 139-140, 149, 155, 159, 165, 171, 173, 175, 177, 185, 187, 197, 207, 211, 217, 227, 235, 237, 241, 245, 247, 251, 253, 257, 261
Savory Batter Bread Master Recipe 93-94
Scones 33, 38, 50, 61-62, 103, 109, 111-113, 211, 257
    Blueberry Lemon 113
    Cherry Almond 113
    Master Recipe 111-113
Score 65-66
Self-rising flour 33-34
Shortbread 130, 133-136, 182, 194, 203, 208, 212
    Crumb Bars 136
    Cut-Out Cookies 134
    Master Recipe 133-136
    Tart or Pie Crust 62, 136, 182, 184, 194, 203 208, 212
    Thumbprint Cookies 135
Shortcake, Strawberry 111, 113, 250
Shortening 35-36, 48, 103, 107, 185, 187
Sift 66, 146,
Soda bread 103, 115-116
    Brown Bread 116
    Currant and Caraway 116
    Master Recipe 115-116
Softened 51, 66
Streusel 89-90, 98, 156, 182, 184, 194, 199, 212-213, 221-222, 261
    Topping Recipe 261
Substitutions 46-49
    Buttermilk 48-49
    Cake flour 49
    Dairy-free 48
    Egg-free 47-48
    Gluten-free 47
Sugar 35, 37-38, 41-43, 46, 50-51, 54, 60-61, 66, 71-73, 89, 93, 97-98, 107, 111-113, 115-116, 120, 123, 127, 130-131, 133, 135-136, 139-140, 149, 152-153, 155, 159, 162-163, 165, 168, 171, 173, 175-177, 185, 187, 193, 195, 197-199, 203, 207, 211-214, 217, 222, 226-227, 233, 241, 245, 247, 250-251, 257, 261, 263
    Role in baking 37

Varieties of 38
Sweet Batter Bread Master Recipe 89-91

T

Temper 66
Toasted Nuts or Coconut 256
Turbinado sugar 38, 98-99, 112-113

V

Vanilla 90-91, 97, 111, 113, 123, 127-128, 133, 139, 149, 155, 159-160, 171-172, 175-177, 197, 203-204, 207, 217, 221, 257-258, 263

W

Whipped cream 50, 63, 113, 155, 166, 178, 182, 200, 208, 213, 221, 263
    topping 263
Whole wheat flour 30, 32, 34, 116, 233, 243

Y

Yeast 31, 33-34, 41, 43, 47, 60, 62-65, 225-230, 232-233, 235, 241-242, 245-247
    About 43, 226
    How it functions 226

Mango Publishing, established in 2014, publishes an eclectic list of books by diverse authors—both new and established voices—on topics ranging from business, personal growth, women's empowerment, LGBTQ studies, health, and spirituality to history, popular culture, time management, decluttering, lifestyle, mental wellness, aging, and sustainable living. We were recently named 2019 *and* 2020's #1 fastest-growing independent publisher by *Publishers Weekly*. Our success is driven by our main goal, which is to publish high -quality books that will entertain readers as well as make a positive difference in their lives.

Our readers are our most important resource; we value your input, suggestions, and ideas. We'd love to hear from you—after all, we are publishing books for you!

Please stay in touch with us and follow us at:

Facebook: Mango Publishing
Twitter: @MangoPublishing
Instagram: @MangoPublishing
LinkedIn: Mango Publishing
Pinterest: Mango Publishing
Newsletter: mangopublishinggroup.com/newsletter

Join us on Mango's journey to reinvent publishing, one book at a time.